KU-436-230

GROWING THINGS

How to Garden without a Garden

Elizabeth Gundrey is the author of another Piccolo book, *Sewing Things*, and of *Fun with Art*, *Fun Food* and *Fun Dressing-up* (all for children). She has written many adult books such as *Go-as-you-please Holidays*, *Your Money's Worth* and *At Your Service*. She used to edit *Shopper's Guide* and now edits the history magazine *Then*, which recreates the past from old newspapers, reports, cartoons, letters, etc.

After studying horticulture at university and working for the magazine *Popular Gardening*, **Janet Browne** helped set up the Syon Park Gardening Centre; six years ago she founded her own public-relations company specializing in horticulture. She also edits the *London Weekly*'s 'Diary of Social Events'.

By the same author in Piccolo

SEWING THINGS

CONDITIONS OF SALE

This book shall not, by way of trade or otherwise, be lent, re-sold, hired out or otherwise circulated without the publisher's prior consent in any form of binding or cover other than that in which it is published and without a similar condition including this condition being imposed on the subsequent purchaser. The book is published at a net price and is supplied subject to the Publishers Association Standard Conditions of Sale registered under the Restrictive Trade Practices Act, 1956.

GROWING THINGS

How to Garden without a Garden

ELIZABETH GUNDREY

Technical consultant, JANET BROWNE

Cover by DAVID DAVIES

Text illustrations by JOHN WOODS

A Piccolo Original

PAN BOOKS LTD
LONDON

First published 1973 by Pan Books Ltd,
33 Tothill Street, London, SW1.

ISBN 0 330 23505 2

2nd Printing 1973

© Elizabeth Gundrey 1973

Printed in Great Britain by
Richard Clay (The Chaucer Press), Ltd,
Bungay, Suffolk

For Sally, Tom and Zannie

Contents

Gardening without a Garden

I have over 100 plants – but no garden.

As this book tells you, there's no need for lots of space in order to be a gardener. Even if you live in a small town flat you can have a go. In fact, high flats often have purer air and more light – two things plants thrive on – than some homes on the ground.

You need to choose the right kind of plants, though. This book describes over a hundred that are suitable, and which can easily be found in small gardening shops and most branches of Woolworth's. But there are many hundreds more. If you go to a specialist plant shop or nursery (you can find them by looking in the yellow pages of a telephone directory), there will be experts there willing to advise you – they will be able to give you more time if you *don't* go at a busy time, like Saturday morning.

Tell them where the plant will be put and the sort of plant you want. Is your home centrally heated (tropical plants will like this) or does it get cold at night? Perhaps you have a balcony or porch, in which case outdoor, not indoor, varieties will be needed: ask which variety is which and find out as much as possible about how to look after them. Some plants grow better in one area than another and it is quite a good idea to notice what grows well in your next-door neighbour's home. Some like a sunny, south-facing windowsill, many prefer a shady, north-facing one. Which way do your windows face?

Nearly everything grows best if you start it off in spring – but there are quite a lot of plants you *can* put in at other times, so hunt through the book for these if you want to start at other seasons.

Visit any nearby botanical gardens and parks (particularly ones with greenhouses) to get ideas. You could even have a chat with the gardeners there, if they are friendly. Some private houses have lovely gardens and open them to the public on certain days.

People who love gardens usually love to share their knowledge with you (and sometimes bits of their plants, too!)

Finally, if you are a forgetful person who may let plants die through lack of watering (or have no one to care for your plants when you're on holiday), have a particular look at Chapters 2, 3, 4 and 6 for some really foolproof ideas.

The other chapters will give you lots of other ideas on how to look after plants, and will show you how easily some of the unusual ones can be grown.

No 1 In the Kitchen

Growing things is easy. So easy that sometimes you can't stop things growing when you want to. Has your mother never found a potato or an onion sprouting away if it has accidentally been left too long in the vegetable rack?

In fact, to find out just how easy growing is, why not start in the kitchen?

Carrots

Here's the nearest thing to instant gardening! You can use any carrot (except one of the packaged kind, which may possibly have been frozen before it reached the shop), or a parsnip or turnip.

Simply slice off the top (you need about ½ inch) and stand it in a saucer with enough water to cover the bottom part, in a nice light spot – unlike human beings, most plants die if they don't get lots of daylight. The water shouldn't cover the carrot-top but simply keep the bottom part moist. Add more water when it begins to dry up.

If the weather isn't cold, within a few days you should see little shoots starting, and after a week or two you should get the beginnings of a lovely plume of feathery leaves 6–8 inches tall. Roots will appear. Carrots are one of the prettiest plants to grow like this, yet all they need is light, a little warmth, and water.

There's another way to grow a carrot or parsnip – upside down!

This time you need a 2-inch piece from the top of a big carrot. Scoop out an inch of the core from the cut end with a sharp little knife or point of a potato-peeler, taking care not to pierce the top. Then stick a small skewer or cocktail stick through both sides, near the cut end, and use this to hang it up on a piece of string like a little basket. Keep the hole filled with water daily. The feathery leaves will start to sprout from the bottom and then grow upwards.

Instead of just water, you could even fill the hole with moist earth and grow a seed or two in it, such as one of the smaller varieties of nasturtium.

Remember that the carrot must hang in a light place (which room in your house gets most daylight?) and don't forget to top up the water every day.

Beetroot

You can grow a beetroot top in a saucer just like a carrot top. But, of course, you must start with a raw beetroot – many sold by the greengrocers have been boiled. In about ten days you will start to get some splendid green leaves with red veins.

Peaches, apricots or nectarines

You can start growing at any time, though in winter results will be slower; in any case, you may have to wait some months.

If a peach stone is very carefully cracked with nutcrackers, just to break it open a little round the sides, and then planted, it

should grow easily and make a little tree. Each spring, cut back the branches to keep it a nice, compact, tree-like shape. You might even get flowers and fruit one day, if the plant is kept in a warm place and moved into a larger pot each spring (*see* pages 114–15).

To plant your fruit stone you will need a flowerpot about four inches deep, and some compost to fill it. Later in this book you can read about composts but for the moment all you need do is go to Woolworth's, a plant shop or even an ironmonger, and ask for a small bag of John Innes Potting Compost No 1. It will cost you a few pence and you will be able to use it for lots of things described in this book.

Before putting compost in the pot, cover the hole at the bottom with a bottle-cap to stop water running out too freely. Put in an inch layer of pebbles and fill the pot to about an inch from the top; press the compost down and put the stone in, covering it with a little more compost. Water well, and do so again whenever the compost begins to feel dry. Stand the pot in a saucer to catch the drips.

If possible, place the pot in a sunny spot outdoors during the summer.

Avocados

That hard stone in the middle of an avocado pear is full of promise, but it needs slightly different care. It doesn't like light at first. Although you can grow it in compost, it is easier and much more interesting to watch if you start it off in water.

Have you got a tumbler of blue or green glass? If so, put the stone in (pointed end up) and pour water in till it is halfway up the stone. Then put it by a warm radiator or stove – not a gas one, as the fumes may harm it. If you haven't got a coloured glass, use an ordinary one but put it in a warm, dark cupboard, or shield it from light with dark paper or kitchen foil. Keep the water topped up. If it and the stone get slimy, rinse the glass and the stone under a tap.

After about 3–6 weeks, you should see the stone begin to split, and both a shoot and a root will start to grow out of the split. When they are about an inch long, transfer the plant to a pot about six inches deep, containing John Innes Compost No 1. The compost should come to about 1 inch below the tip of the stone.

Now keep the avocado in a warm, shady place, looking at it every two or three days to check that the compost hasn't got dry and to see whether the shoot is growing upwards properly.

As soon as it is 2–3 inches high, put the plant in a light place and it will start growing very fast: you may end up with a 6-foot giant! But this will probably take 3–4 years, depending on the amount of sunshine it gets. It will also need a much larger pot later, and, to help it keep upright, a thin stick which you should push into the compost in the pot and tie to the stem. If you don't want a tall plant, leave it in the small pot and this will stunt its growth.

What the grown-up avocado wants most is plenty of light, especially in winter, but its need for warmth will not be so great as in its early days. Keep it out of draughts, though. And, in summer, add a little fertilizer (*see* page 28) to the water you give it. It should be watered whenever the compost feels dry.

Pineapple

Cut the top off just below the leaves and put in a pot (6 inches deep) full of damp sand, with a polythene bag over the top. In several months, it may grow roots and new leaves if you're lucky.

Oranges and lemons

. . . and grapefruit and tangerines and mandarins. All these are

called citrus fruits, and you treat their pips the same way. The best time to start is spring.

Pips are simply seeds, and growing things from seeds takes time – so don't try if you haven't any patience!

Fill some pots (3–4 inches deep) with John Innes Compost No 1, and water them well. Press three pips into each pot – about ½ inch down. Don't put different fruits into one pot, because they grow at different speeds. (Instead of pots you could use the skins of oranges cut in half.)

Keep the pots in a fairly warm, dark place like an airing cupboard (or in any warm place but shielded from the light with, for instance, kitchen foil over the top: if you use this method, turn the foil daily to air it). Check every few days that the compost is still moist. When shoots appear above the surface, in 1–2 months, put the pots in a shady place for a few days and then in a light one. During summer they can stand outdoors in a warm corner.

When the plants are about 4 inches high, each should be put into its own bigger pot of compost: do this changeover very gently as it could kill the plant if you broke its roots. Two or three months later, you should find you have some little glossy-leaved trees growing (and, if you wait a few years, you might even get some little flowers and tiny fruit on a tree about 4–6 feet high). For bigger plants, change to a 14–16-inch pot in the second or third spring.

Cut off the tops of new shoots each spring to keep the tree round and bushy. Water it, and add fertilizer, as needed.

Dates

Date-stones are tricky and difficult to please: you may or may not get results with them. But if you live in a home with central heating or a hot-water tank, it's worth having a try at producing a palm-tree in a pot if you're prepared to wait 3–6 months.

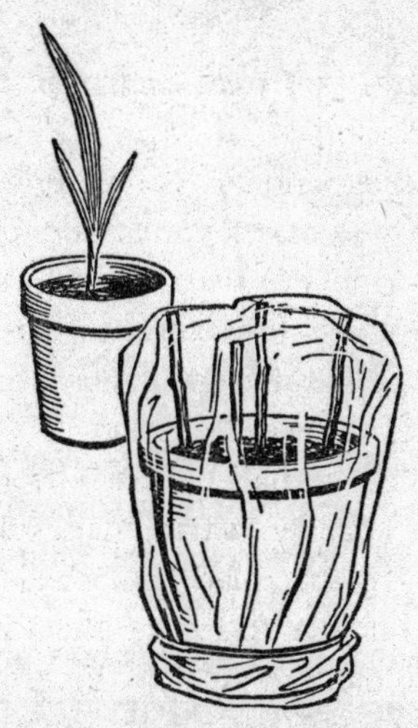

Dates need lots of heat (think of the Sahara and India where they grow) so, having planted them in the same way as the orange pips, stand the pot on a radiator or hot tank. Keep a polythene bag over the pot until shoots appear (you can keep it erect with a couple of twigs or sticks stuck in the compost, and a rubber-band round the bottom – see drawing). This is to protect the plant from draughts and keep the air round it moist.

Be sure to keep the compost damp (but not squelchy-wet).

When the plants are 3 inches high you can put them in separate pots, without bags. Keep them in a warm place, water regularly and in summer add a little fertilizer (*see* page 28) to the water.

Mangoes and lychees

These are two very exotic fruits which you can sometimes buy in greengrocers'. Both are delicious to eat, and have stones that

produce dramatic plants quite quickly. Very few people try to grow them, so if you do you will have something special to show.

Lychees are prickly, brown-skinned fruit on a twig (3–4 per twig), and if you pull the shell off, inside is a white juicy substance to eat. Inside that is a brown stone, about an inch long.

Mangoes are big, orange-green fruit with shiny skins. You eat the juicy flesh (preferably in the bath because they are very squidgy) and inside is a very large, hard, woody stone.

Grow these stones just like avocados. They'll take 1–3 months to start growing. The lychee can give you about 6 feet of stem with green leaves in its first year, while the mango will produce a plant which at first will have the most fantastic contortions. Then it grows about a foot a year, with lovely long green leaves. A very jungly pair to have about the house.

Both like warm, moist places and must never get cold. Provided it does not go cold at night, a steamy bathroom or kitchen would be most like the tropical conditions they come from. They love central heating but must be kept moist.

Onions

These sound rather humdrum after the tropical splendours of mangoes and lychees. But they do have a very handsome flower – provided your family don't complain about the oniony smell that goes with it.

Simply plant the onion (point uppermost) in a pot about 6 inches deep containing John Innes Compost No 1, which should come a third of the way up the onion. Water occasionally, and await results. If planted about February, in about 4 months you should get a biggish globe of mauve flowers on the end of a stalk about 1½ feet tall (it will probably need tying to a stick to stop it toppling over). If you have a garden, when the flower is dead hang it upside down to dry. The seeds in the head could then be planted next spring and put out in the garden to grow and make new bulbs.

As always, remember the plant will need light and water (but not too much) if it is to flourish.

Potatoes

The homely spud will give you a really big indoor creeper with no more help than a jar of water. You need to start it off in the spring.

Find a large jar with a top, that will just fit the potato (which should be an *old* one), or make a cardboard collar to hold it – *see* page 21. Perch the potato in it so that as many 'eyes' as possible are at the top and with water reaching halfway up it. ('Eyes' are the little black spots.) Keep topping the water up whenever it falls below this level.

Put the jar in a cool, dark cupboard.

As soon as you can see roots growing down, bring the jar out into the light. If lots of green shoots appear, cut off all except two. This means the potato will put all its energy into just these two and they may grow as long as 6 feet in 3–4 months, particularly if you add a little liquid fertilizer to the water and can stand the plant in a light spot. If you want a lower, bushy plant, don't remove any of the shoots.

To help the plant climb, fasten two strings to the wall and tie the shoots to them.

Baby potatoes can grow on the roots but you need a very big jar to hold them. If you want to eat them, no light should reach

the little potatoes, to keep them white. If the light gets at them, they will be green and bad to eat.

You can even get a mini-creeper which will grow from just one tiny bit of potato (with one or more 'eyes' on it) placed in a saucer of water.

Mustard and cress

Here's one with a crop you can really eat! You need one packet of mustard seeds and one of cress.

Put some squares of wet, absorbent kitchen-paper on a plate and sprinkle on enough cress seeds from the packet to cover the surface (but be sure no seeds are on top of others). Cover the seeds with another piece of paper – dry – or a piece of foil, or a second plate. Three days later, on a separate plate with wet paper, scatter mustard seeds in the same way and cover them. Keep the papers moist but not sopping wet. When the seeds have produced tiny roots and shoots, you remove the covering.

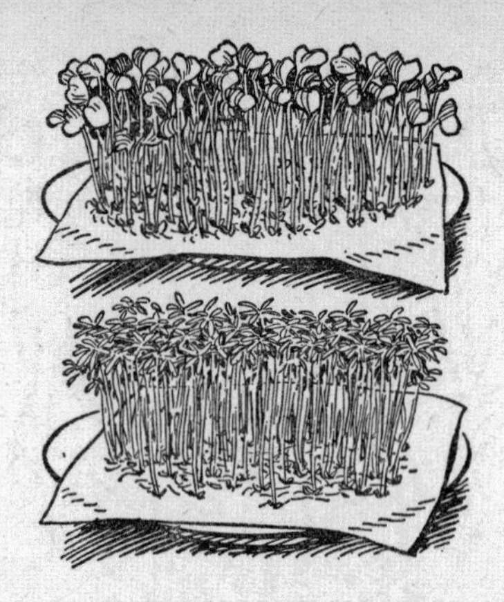

If the plates are in a sunny spot (indoors or out), in two weeks after sowing you can cut the mustard and the cress (now $2\frac{1}{2}$ or 3 inches high) with scissors, rinse under the tap, mix, and eat in sandwiches or salad.

As the packets contain lots more seeds, you can keep on doing this with fresh pieces of wet paper.

Mint

Next time your mother buys some mint for cooking, take a sprig, cut it just below one pair of leaves and put it in water in a light place. It will grow roots and start a whole new plant: a useful present to give her.

Chinese bean-shoots

Do you like eating in Chinese restaurants? Then you probably enjoy eating bean-shoots. The restaurants often grow them in their kitchens – and so can you.

You do it in much the same way as mustard and cress, but be sure to get the right kind of seeds – they're called Mung Beans and you can buy them at seed shops. The packet will carry precise instructions for growing the seeds.

When you've cut your crop of bean-shoots 10–14 days later,

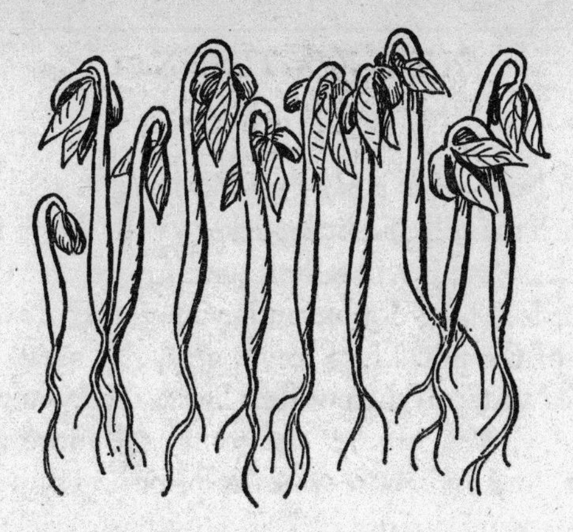

cook them in boiling water with ½ teaspoon of salt for only 2 minutes.

Melons, marrows and cucumbers

Quick-growing plants if you start in spring. Treat the pips just like the citrus ones, but keep them in a rather warmer place. After 3–6 weeks you will get little plants and later very decorative creepers which, with the help of drawing-pins and string, you can train to grow round a window, up a wall, etc. In about a year you may have plants 4 feet long!

QUESTION TIME No 1

WATERING

How do you know when a plant needs watering?
Lightly touch the soil. If a little sticks to your finger it is damp enough. If it is dry, it will fall off your finger, and this means water is needed. If in doubt, push your finger down ¼ inch at the side of the pot. Limp leaves generally mean a plant is desperate for water. If the pot feels light when you pick it up, the soil is dry. The warmer the room, the more often you must water. And give more water in spring and summer when a plant is growing rapidly or is in flower.

How much water should you give it?
Stand the pot on a saucer and gently pour water on the soil (not on the plant) till it runs out at the bottom. After ¼ hour, empty the saucer. Most plants drink mainly through their roots, so the water must get down to the bottom. Occasionally, if the soil gets dry, soak the whole pot in a sink of water, leave for ¼ hour, then drain before putting back on its saucer. In warm conditions you can spray the leaves: use a clean plastic squeezy bottle.

Can a plant have too much water?
Yes – and this could kill it. The roots will rot, and the leaves will turn yellow and drop off. Plants don't like puddles or mud – unless they're water-weeds! Twice a week in summer and once a week in winter suits most indoor plants. Plants with thick fleshy leaves need even less water.

And use proper flowerpots with a hole in the bottom. In an ordinary bowl, water collects at the bottom and can rot the roots. You can make proper little pots by piercing holes in the bottom of plastic cream or yogurt cartons – use a heated skewer to do this. Never use icy-cold water.

No 2 Gardening Without Soil

If you live in a flat, it may be difficult to get hold of soil to grow plants in. You can always buy a bag of compost, of course – but there is another way which will save your pocket-money. And it's less messy.

In the last chapter, several odds-and-ends from the kitchen were growing quite happily in water. Lots more plants can be grown like that and kept indefinitely – almost anything except the few (such as cacti) that positively hate wetness. This method is called soilless culture, or hydroponics. It is sometimes used to grow crops in deserts, and there are even plans to use it on the moon to give colonies of astronauts fresh vegetables.

Friends with flourishing indoor plants are usually very happy to cut you a leaf or stem, or a piece of root; you can then get these cuttings to grow in a jar of water instead of a pot of soil until they too produce roots and turn into flourishing plants.

On pages 30–32 are pictures and details of some very suitable ones to try, because they usually grow particularly quickly and easily, but you can try many others too.

All you need to start with is a glass jar, water, a piece of thin cardboard and, later, fertilizer. In the case of larger bulbs such as hyacinths, you won't need the cardboard.

Cut out a disc a little larger than the mouth of the jar, then cut a criss-cross in the centre and open this up just enough to hold the cutting or plant with its leaves above and its stem below, hanging in the water.

If you have a very tiny cutting, a small bottle may be better than a jar, with a cork instead of the cardboard lid. Cut the cork in half lengthways and slice a little off one half. Then put the stalk between the two halves before replacing the cork lightly in the bottle. But don't squash the stalk.

Because roots like darkness, cut a piece of thin card, coloured paper or cooking foil to go round the jar, and hold it in place with paper-clips. If you use card or paper, you could paint a decorative pattern. Remove this covering only to check occasionally whether the water needs topping up or to see how the roots are growing. If your jar or bottle is made of coloured glass, you do not need to put paper round.

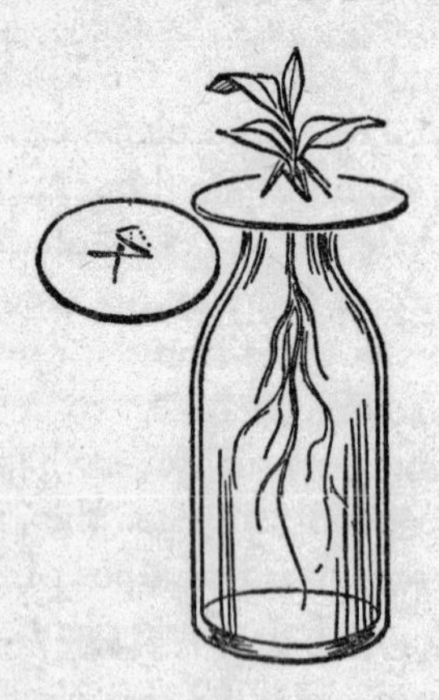

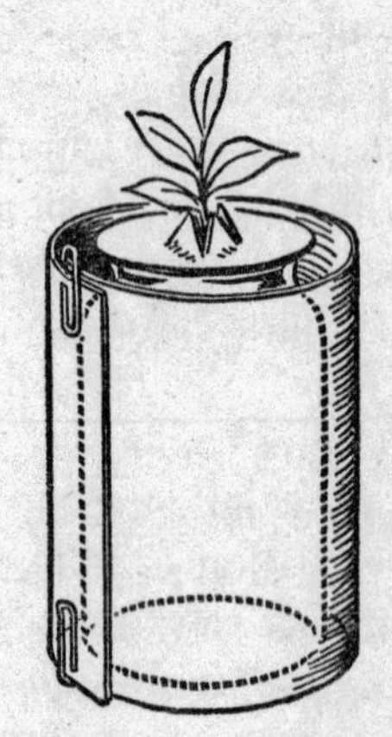

Many plants will live and grow happily like this for several weeks if you give them as much or as little light as they need. If they are plants that like warmth, put them in a warm place (but never over an open fire); if they dislike sunshine, keep them away from it – in fact, do just what you would if they were growing in soil. This book tells you the likes and dislikes of every plant mentioned in it, and it's important to choose plants that will like the spot where you're planning to put them. Remember that a warm room by day may become icy at night, especially near the window; or may be subject to chilly draughts if a door is in frequent use (*see* page 29). Different plants, if they have the same likes and dislikes, can grow in one jar.

The really great thing about soilless gardening of this kind is that you don't have to resist that awful temptation to pull the plants up in order to see whether they're growing roots or not.

After one or more weeks, you should be able to see them in the water. Some will be fleshy and some like fine hairs, some long and some short – it depends on the plant. And having seen the roots that grow in water, when you grow plants in soil you will be able to imagine what their roots are doing underneath the soil.

After a few weeks you will probably need to give the plant a little fertilizer in its water, and it may by now be too big to stay where it is.

Small plants and trailing ones can often be kept in the same jar for ages (with fertilizer added – *see* page 28), changing the water every month or so. Do this carefully so as not to disturb the roots too much. If the leaves are dusty, wipe them with damp cotton-wool.

A big plant needs more support and food than just water – something to anchor the roots so that they can keep the top part of the plant steady and feed it. If you are going to grow plants this way, you need two containers – an inner one with at least one hole in it (like a flowerpot), and an outer one. The inner one will contain something to hold the roots, and can be lifted out when you want to change the water (about every month) without disturbing the roots any more. The outer container holds the water and fertilizer which, of course, gets through to the roots because the inner pot has a hole in it. The inner pot can have in it what is called aggregate – pebbles, gravel, very small bits of rock and stone, or the chippings which pet shops sell for fish-tanks. Vermiculite, sold for gardening or for attic insulation, is another suitable thing, or coarse sand. Wash these well first (remember sand from the sea-shore is salty): soak in hot water, then put in a sieve or old stocking under the cold tap. Don't use anything in the container that might rot, like bits of wood; or anything which might have chemicals in it that could kill plants.

Put some pebbles in the bottom of the pot, then hold the plant in position. Gently add the aggregate little by little (taking care not to damage the roots), until it is an inch from the top of the pot. Stand the pot in the outer bowl, and fill it up with water containing fertilizer (letting some flow over into the outer bowl).

The best fertilizer for this purpose is either a liquid or a powder that dissolves in water. Phostrogen was especially formulated for the purpose and is cheap. If you can't find it use Bio Plant Food, Maxicrop or Suttons House Plant Food No 4. These fertilizers are not poisonous and they contain the right food for most plants. The labels tell you how much to add

– less in winter than in spring or summer. The best method is to mix the fertilizer into water in a jug and then pour this into the pot when topping up the water or when renewing it completely. Every 7–10 days you should carefully pour plain water through the contents of the inner pot, throw away any liquid in the outer bowl, and start again with a fresh lot of water and fertilizer.

You can also sow seeds, root cuttings and grow bulbs by this method, but use only a very little fertilizer to start with, making it stronger as the plants grow.

For more information read *Beginner's Guide to Hydroponics* by J. Sholto Douglas (Pelham Books) and free leaflet No 11 from Phostrogen Ltd, Corwen, Merioneth LL21 0EE.

Where house plants should be put

This drawing shows whereabouts in a room most plants are likely to grow best.

√ *GENERALLY GOOD SPOTS*

Light-loving plants near the window.
Shade-loving ones farther in.

× *RISKY SPOTS*

Windowsill. For some plants, it may be too sunny in summer. For all, it may be too cold and draughty at night in winter.
Mantelpiece. For most plants, too hot when fire is lit. For some, gas fumes are harmful.
Near door. Many plants hate draughts.

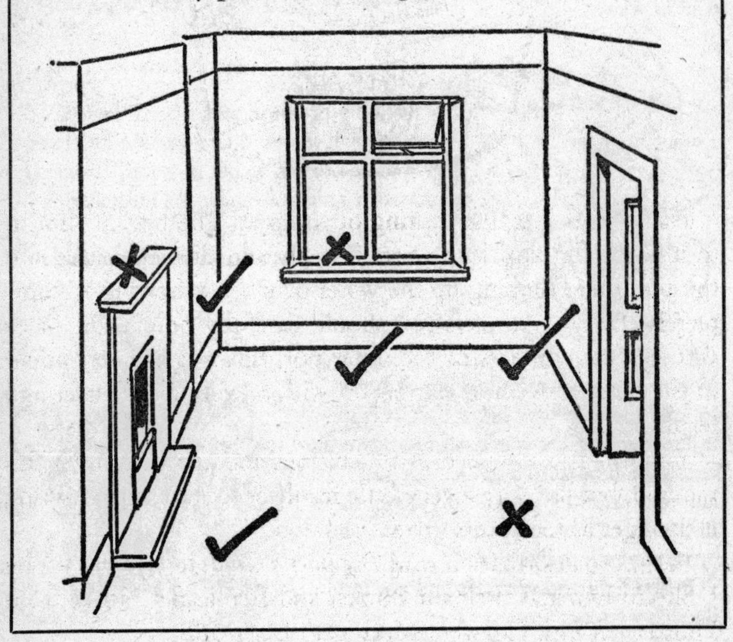

Some plants to grow without soil

Ask a friend who has any of these plants if you may have a cutting or plant to put in water (or, in the case of crocuses and hyacinths, buy bulbs). Put each new plant in a room that will suit it, and follow the water and fertilizer instructions given previously.

BEGONIA — *Begonia*

Some have fibrous roots and some have tubers (bulbs). Fibrous ones produce red, pink or white flowers in spring or autumn. Tuberous ones have all sorts of colours, flowering in summer or autumn. A begonia can be grown in water if it has roots (rinse them first to remove any soil).

It likes a light, sunny room which is not cold in winter.

BUSY LIZZIE — *Impatiens*

It busily produces pink or red flowers nearly all the year. Can grow a lot. Take a piece of stem to put in water, cutting it with a knife just under the little bump below a pair of leaves.

It likes a place that is sunny and fairly warm.

CROCUS — *Crocus*

You need a small-mouthed pot or bottle to hold the little bulb on so that its base is just touching the water. Spring-flowering ones should be started in October and autumn-flowering ones in July. Keep them in the dark till roots appear. You can also grow snowdrops like this.

It likes light and warmth, and not too draughty a spot.

GERANIUM *Pelargonium*

Brilliant red, pink or white flowers that last a long time. Some have multi-coloured leaves. Cut a piece of stem in spring or autumn, below a pair of leaves, to put in water. Use plenty of fertilizer in spring and summer.

It likes lots of light and sun.

HYACINTH *Hyacinthus*

Pink, blue, red, yellow or white flowers, with a lovely scent. Buy a bulb in autumn, sit it on a jar with a mouth that fits it, with water not quite touching. Keep in dark till roots appear. You can also grow tulips and daffodils like this, provided you choose varieties that have short stems, as tall ones may topple over.

It likes a room that is light, warm and draught-free.

IVY *Hedera*

Lots of varieties, some with two-coloured leaves, with stems that climb up or hang down. Take a short length with a bit of root on it to put in water. Inconspicuous flowers.

It likes to be cool, not hot and dry. Ivies with multi-coloured leaves need more light.

MOTHER-OF-THOUSANDS

Saxifraga sarmentosa

A little plant with round, hairy leaves (reddish underneath). Tiny flowers. It sends out thread-like stems with baby leaves at the ends: take one to put in water.

It likes coolness and light but not too much sun.

SPIDER PLANT *Chlorophytum*

Long, grassy leaves with stripes. Tiny white flowers. It sends out long thin stems with little 'spiders' of tiny leaves on them. Take one 'spider' to start a new plant.

It likes a light and airy place, but not sunny. This plant doesn't mind gas fumes.

WANDERING JEW *Tradescantia* and *Zebrina*

Two plants share this name, both usually with striped, pointed leaves on wandering stems. Zebrina leaves are more silky, and purple underneath. Put a stem of either in water.

It likes to be cool and not too sunny.

QUESTION TIME No 2

PLANTS' NAMES

Why do plants have more than one name?
Most plants have at least two names. They usually have at least one common name in English (sometimes more), such as fig, and they have a Latin name, in this case *Ficus.*

When there are many kinds of the same sort of plant, each of these is given a second name (usually in Latin) to distinguish them from one another. *Ficus elastica* is the kind of fig known as indiarubber plant. *Ficus pumila* is the climbing fig. *Ficus benjamina* is the weeping fig. (For brevity, these names are sometimes written *F. elastica*, etc.) You can think of *Ficus* as the family surname and *elastica*, *pumila* and *benjamina* as Christian names. Sometimes, like people, plants have a second Christian name, like *F. elastica decora* which has more decorative leaves than plain *F. elastica.*

Why bother with Latin names?
They're useful if you want to be certain of buying a particular variety. The English names have become muddled with time – for instance, the fig-leaf palm is neither a fig nor a palm! Plants from the same family sometimes look quite different, and have different likes and dislikes. So you will find both English and Latin names in this book.

No 3 Gardens in Bottles

Here's another way to have a garden of your own indoors, particularly if you're forgetful about watering pot-plants. You can begin one at any time, though spring is best.

To start with you need the biggest glass jar you can get with an opening at least two inches across. A gallon-size cider flagon would do, or perhaps you could persuade a local sweetshop to let you have cheaply one of their huge glass jars. Some ironmongers sell big glass, or transparent plastic, kitchen storage jars, round or square, for 25p to 65p. An old goldfish bowl would do, and

some goods are sold in transparent plastic packs that could be used. Or, for just one tiny plant, try a large wineglass or glass mug.

If you are going to use a container that once had something else in it, wash every trace out and dry thoroughly.

If the container hasn't got a stopper or lid, this doesn't matter, but don't try to use a narrow bottle, nor a coloured glass jar.

You need to buy a bag of charcoal chips from a gardening

or hardware shop (or charcoal tablets from a chemist) as well as some John Innes Compost No 2.

Cut out a half-circle of kitchen foil or paper and fold it round into a cone, then snip the bottom off. You now have a funnel through which to pour first the charcoal (to make a layer an inch deep) and then the compost into the bottle.

How much compost to use depends on the size of the jar. You want it to be one-third full before you put the plants in.

The purpose of the charcoal is to absorb any excess of water or 'sourness' that may occur later, because the jar has no drainage hole. You are not likely to use up all the charcoal you have bought, but it will come in handy for other purposes described later in this book.

Now comes the tricky part – getting the plants in. But first: which plants?

Inside the jar there will be a fairly moist, warm atmosphere. But there probably won't be room for anything that grows a lot. Plants which like these conditions include three that were discussed in the last chapter: ivy, spider plant and wandering Jew. Others, discussed on pages 38–40, are:

Fittonia (small)	Aluminium plant
Coconut palm	Mother-in-law's tongue
Pepper elder	Croton
African violet (small)	Cyclamen

You can also put in any small indoor ferns you like.

Don't attempt to put garden plants in – the atmosphere will be wrong for most of them and you might accidentally put in some weeds too. It is better not to put in a fully grown plant, but young ones with roots, from your own or friends' plants (in the case of the cyclamens you need to buy corms – bulbs). They will soon grow bigger.

You could make a bottle-garden with nothing but cacti in it (these are described in the chapter on desert gardens) but don't attempt to mix cacti and other plants because they need different amounts of water.

To put the plants in if the jar has a narrow mouth, fasten the smallest spoon you can find to a stick – Sellotape may be easier to use than string. Insert this through the top of the jar and, very carefully, dig a small hole towards one side – but not so close to the glass that the plant's leaves will touch this.

Taking the smallest plant first, drop it in (roots first) through

the top. Using the spoon, gently push it into the hole and tap the compost firm around it. Do the same with the rest – the tallest plant should go in last and be put in a hole in the middle.

By now, some compost will probably have got spattered on the glass inside. To clean it off, fasten a little bit of damp sponge or cotton-wool onto the end of a piece of bent wire and wiggle this round inside.

Finally, just trickle (don't pour) tepid water in till the compost is really damp – but not soggy.

Put the stopper in, if there is one, and stand the jar in a light, fairly warm, spot.

If you like, for about 35p you can buy a special electric lamp-holder to replace the stopper, and then you could have a lightbulb (with shade) on top shining down onto your garden. The plants will enjoy the light and you will have a very attractive table lamp.

Stand the jar where it is neither very sunny nor very cold.

After that, you have almost nothing more to do. Just add a little water round the edges of the jar once or twice a year when the soil at the edge of the glass looks dry; or more often if there is no stopper in the jar. The plants in an enclosed jar water themselves, because no moisture is lost; it is continually re-used. You may notice the glass occasionally covered in 'dew' if the room gets cool, and then it clears itself again as the plants re-absorb the moisture.

If any leaves turn yellow and die, or plants grow too big, you can cut them with a razor-blade fastened to a stick and remove the debris by means of long tongs made from a piece of bamboo split halfway down the middle; or a long, sharp pickle-fork or skewer.

AFRICAN VIOLET *Saintpaulia*

Named after Baron St Paul, who discovered it. Purple flowers (or sometimes pink or white) like primroses, which keep on appearing for months. Plushy leaves, green on top, reddish below. You can grow a new plant from just one leaf and its stem. Never put water on the leaves as this turns them brown.

It likes warmth and a little light, without draughts or gas fumes, and likes a moist atmosphere, as in a bathroom.

ALUMINIUM PLANT *Pilea*

This gets its name from the silvery pattern on its green leaves, which are about three inches long. A cutting is enough to start a new plant, or the roots can be divided.

It likes warmth, and protection from draughts and gas fumes, but is happy in either light or shade.

COCONUT PALM

Cocos (Syagrus) weddeliana

A very small, graceful palm. Coco is Portuguese for monkey: the palm grows from a nut that looks like a monkey's face. It grows about a foot high (or more) but is not easy to start, so buy a little plant.

It likes plenty of light and no draughts.

CROTON *Codiaeum*

The leaves, which grow to 4–5 inches, have a mixture of green and red-yellow colours. A shrubby and attractive plant.

It likes warmth and moisture, with plenty of light and no draughts.

CYCLAMEN (Hardy)
Cyclamen neapolitanum

The name means 'a circle', for the stem curves round. It grows from a little tuber (bulb) into a plant only four inches high, with prettily shaped pink or white flowers in autumn. Both stem and roots grow out of the *top* of the tuber (it's important to plant it right way up, with the little hollow on top, about half an inch deep).

It likes little warmth and will flourish in either light or shade.

FITTONIA *Fittonia*

Named after two Victorian sisters who were botanists, this is a creeping plant with red veins all over its dark-green leaves, which are about four inches long. A new plant can be created from one young shoot cut from its parent.

It likes a warm moist place, free from draughts, and without much light.

MOTHER-IN-LAW'S TONGUE

Sanseveria

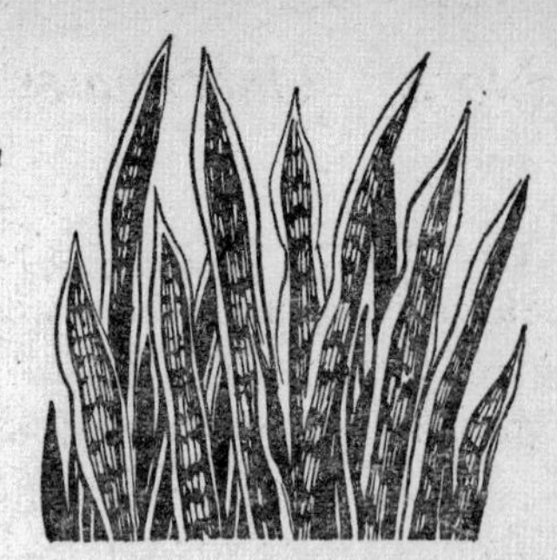

Slim, erect, leathery leaves over a foot tall, with stripes and bands of light and dark green. It rarely flowers. You can start one off by planting a single leaf. Don't give it much water.

It likes warmth and light.

PEPPER ELDER *Peperomia*

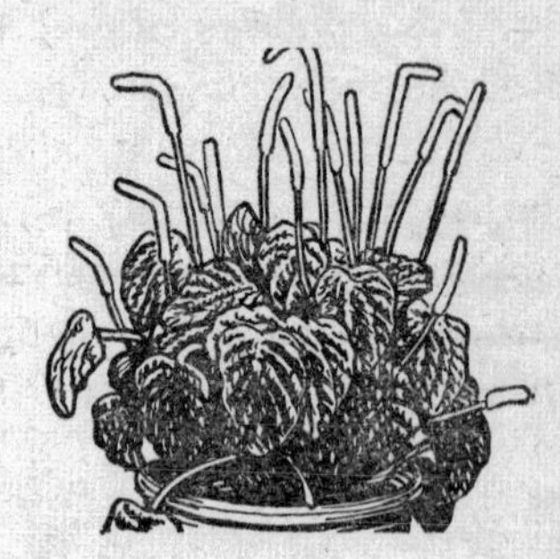

The heart-shaped, tiny, dark-green or mottled leaves are sometimes crinkled all over; and the flowers (which appear in autumn) are like tiny white pipe-cleaners on red stems. It can survive on very little soil or water. You can plant just one leaf and stem to start a new plant growing.

It likes a warm atmosphere without draughts, and lots of light (though not direct sunshine).

No 4 Underwater Gardens

You may not want to go so far as to keep tropical fish, and it is expensive to heat the water for them, but it is still possible to have the next best thing – an indoor cold-water garden. This should be started during summertime.

Once more, you begin with the biggest container of clear plastic or glass you can find (but, unlike the bottle-garden ones, it needs a wide-open top). It must be at least 6 inches deep and 8 inches wide if you want to grow more than one plant. An exception is the plant called anacharis (*see* page 42) which will be happy in a dish only 2–3 inches deep. The container should be absolutely clean. Fish-tanks are ideal: they cost £1 upwards but can occasionally be bought cheaply in junk shops. Some ironmongers sell transparent plastic food-boxes: a big one (about 9″×6″) might cost 40p, a round cake-box less. Or you could have several large jars in a row, with a different plant in each.

If you are good at making things, you could construct a tank yourself, making a bag of very strong transparent plastic sheeting (ask for 1,000 gauge – you buy it from ironmongers or

ANACHARIS *Elodea canadensis*
Dark-green tiny leaves are fanned in a dense mass on brittle stems. Cut it back occasionally to stop it overgrowing other plants.

BOG ARUM *Calla palustris*
Shiny, heart-shaped leaves and sometimes white, lily-like flowers, followed by red berries. Six inches tall.

FAIRY MOSS *Azolla carolina*
This one floats on the surface and has no roots. A fern with tiny leaves that often turn from green to bronze.

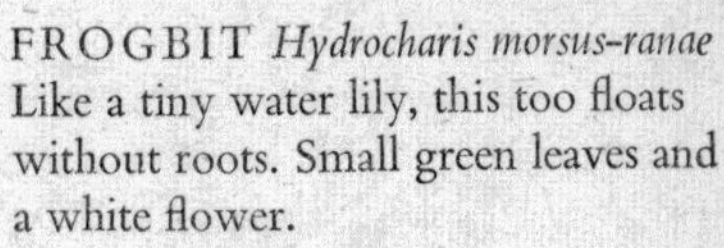

FROGBIT *Hydrocharis morsus-ranae*
Like a tiny water lily, this too floats without roots. Small green leaves and a white flower.

MARE'S TAIL *Hippuris vulgaris*
Thick leaves which rise out of the water like groups of little fir trees. Nine inches tall.

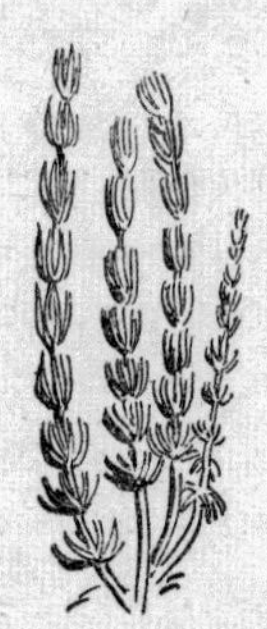

WATER FRINGE *Villarsia nymphaeoides*
Small floating leaves like a water lily and masses of golden flowers. Needs a sunny position and at least 6 inches of water to grow well. (The others can manage with 3 inches.)

builders' merchants) attached to the top of a wooden frame with drawing-pins, in whatever size you like.

The tank should be kept in a spot that gets plenty of light but not sunshine, and where it is not too hot. Cover the bottom first with an inch layer of John Innes Compost No 1 and then with an inch of gravel or coarse sand (rinsed well to remove dust), or chips which you can buy from pet-shops. Put the underwater plants in, with the biggest at the back, and very gently cover their roots with more compost and gravel 3 inches deep. Find some stones and little rocks which are an attractive colour and shape, and put these in to add interest to the scene. You can add seashells if you thoroughly wash all trace of salt water off them. Now very gently pour in water to about 2 inches from the top.

You can also have plants that float on the surface, and these are simply added at the end. They throw shadows on the bottom of the tank, which the underwater plants like and, as they help to keep green algae away, it is worth buying a few. (Algae make the green pea-soup stuff that forms a scum on top of water.)

It is a good idea to add a goldfish or two if you can and are willing to feed them regularly (with special goldfish food), as they eat any insect pests that might attack the plants and make the water-garden look more lively. But they aren't essential. You could also put in a few water-snails, which don't need feeding and, unlike goldfish (which it is cruel to keep in small or circular jars), they can live in even a little container if there are plants. You should not need to change the water, but keep it up to the original level.

If the water does turn green at the start, it should be left to clear itself, which it should do if you have the mixture of plants recommended here, and a few snails.

For not much money you should be able to get all the plants you need. If you had a fish tank about 1¼ feet long and 1 foot across, as in the drawing, you could accommodate perhaps four underwater plants and two floating ones, with two or three snails and two goldfish: all obtainable at pet shops.

If you are feeling very extravagant, or someone will give you a more expensive plant, there is a lovely miniature water-lily called *Pygmaea helvola* which will grow happily in a dish a foot wide and 4 inches deep. It should have 2 inches of compost in the bottom in which to plant the roots, then add water to an inch from the top of the dish. Placed in sunlight, this water-lily with mottled leaves will produce its flowers in a lovely yellow for many months in summer and autumn. It can be grown completely on its own and the water should keep clear and only need occasional topping-up. You can buy it from a water-garden specialist such as Highlands Water Gardens, Ricksmansworth, Herts, or Perry's Hardy Plant Farm, Enfield, Middlesex.

No 5 Hanging Gardens

These are very pretty and take up no standing space. You could hang a small one indoors from the middle of a curtain track if it doesn't get in the way of the curtains, so that it gets plenty of light from the window; or from a bracket screwed to the wall. An outdoor one could hang in a porch, from a wall-bracket or from the underside of a balcony on the floor above you, or from a tree. Remember that you have got to be able to get at it for watering and other purposes; and that the spot you choose must have the amount of light and warmth needed by whatever plants you put in.

You need to buy a wire plant-basket, and this, with chains or wire to hang it, will cost 25p or more (depending on size and whether the wire is plastic-covered or not). You could make do with an old colander, a small bird-cage or even a basket lined with plastic or kitchen foil, perhaps painting the outside with enamel for a fresh look. Woolworth's sell the plant-baskets, not only circular hanging ones but half-circles to fasten to a wall or sides of a balcony (no chains).

The basket has to be lined. You could collect moss from the woods, or buy dried moss from Woolworth's or a gardening shop. Another way is to line it with sacking or else with plastic or foil (use the latter folded in two for extra strength). Moss looks nicest and most natural. If you use plastic or foil, put mostly trailing plants in the basket so that these will later conceal it – or puncture a few holes in the plastic and push the roots of some plants through. Whatever you use to line the basket, there must be holes in the bottom to allow moisture to drain out.

Half fill the basket with John Innes Compost – No 2 is better for this purpose than No 1 because it has more soil and fertilizer in it. But No 1 will do if you intend growing short-lived plants (annuals) which you will throw out at the end of summer. Mix in with the compost some charcoal chips (as described on pages 34–5) to absorb moisture.

Then pack the plants in firmly, pressing more compost down over their roots. Pour plenty of water on (gently) and leave the basket in a cool place for two or three days before putting it in its final position. Water it each morning during this period; and after that, at least once a week pour on enough water to wet the soil thoroughly. The water should contain liquid fertilizer (see page 28). Or you can take the basket off its chains and soak it in a sink of water instead – let it drain before re-hanging it.

Remember with an indoor basket to put a bowl or some newspaper on the floor below to catch the drips after watering.

It is better not to hang a basket in a very sunny place unless you are prepared to water it daily, so choose plants that don't need too much sunshine. And don't hang it in a draughty place because this, too, will dry up the compost.

Pick off any dead flowers or leaves when you do the watering; this will encourage new ones to come along.

You can plant almost anything (except six-foot sunflowers!) in a basket but, because it is overhead, plants that hang down look prettiest, and some may be persuaded also to climb up the chains. Big flowers will show up better than little ones.

For an indoor basket you could use a mixture of some of the perennial (ie, permanent) plants discussed in Chapter 2: mother-of-thousands, wandering Jew, spider plant, ivy, busy Lizzie, aluminium plant, African violet, pepper elder or Christmas cactus (*see* Chapter 6), and also asparagus fern (*see* page 49). You could add a little vase of flowers for colour.

For an outdoor one there is a big choice of flowering plants which trail, for instance, bell flower, lobelia and periwinkle – white and blue flowers which will grow well in a fairly shady position. Bell flowers and periwinkle will live on year after year; lobelia is an annual which flowers only one year. All are described at the end of the chapter.

If you prefer pinks and reds, a somewhat larger basket could contain fuchsias (ask for a small-growing, hardy type) and cranesbills – true geraniums – with some ivy to trail down: see descriptions at the end of this chapter. These, too, would be content in the shade though they do even better in sunshine, and they go on from year to year if kept sheltered from frost. If you want to change the arrangement occasionally, you could put plants in separate pots within the basket, packing moss about them.

However, if the plants you choose for your basket are all annuals or bedding plants (that is to say, they flower during their first year only), at the end of their time you could remove them and use the same compost to create a basket of spring flowers, by planting bulbs in the autumn (*see* Chapter 8). But as these do not trail down, the basket must not be too high or you will not see them. You could add a little ivy around the edges.

Finally, here are some other ways to house plants if you have a little space:

Line the wire baskets of a vegetable rack in the way described above and plant things in these – shade-loving ones at the bottom.

Use an old saucepan rack to stand pots of plants on.

Fasten pots to a wall or the sides of a window or balcony (use either masonry nails or picture nails, plus wire).

Fasten to a wall (with picture nails or, if weighty, Rawlplugs and screws) a kitchen storage rack made of wire, and put a row of pots in it.

If you have a balcony or stairs with railings, pots can be held on these with wire or plastic insulating-tape.

Remember that, if you use such things indoors, you will have to put a pan or newspaper underneath to catch drips when you water the plants.

Some plants for hanging baskets

ASPARAGUS FERN *Asparagus plumosus*
Feathery plumes, light green, which you can cut and add to a vase of flowers. They can grow as long as ten feet, but can be cut back before that.

It likes to be indoors, and is happy in either light or shade.

BELL FLOWER *Campanula isophylla*
Trailing stems with white or blue bell-shaped flowers, quite big. It will last from year to year if you keep it out of frost, and in spring you can cut a stem off and plant it to make a new one, or divide the roots.* Give plenty of water in summer, little in winter.

It likes light or shade, indoors or out.

CRANESBILL *Geranium*
A trailing or upright plant with masses of small leaves and lots of pink or red flowers all through the summer. To get more plants you just divide it up in the spring.* It does not need much water.

It likes some sun but will grow in shade.

* *See* 'How to divide one plant into two', page 110.

FUCHSIA *Fuchsia*

Named after a sixteenth-century botanist, Professor Fuchs, this has very decorative red and purple flowers, often with white or yellow centres, on long stems. It will live from year to year if you keep it out of the frost during winter. When it starts growing again in spring, cut off each stem just above the bottom bud. Don't put it outdoors again until the weather is mild. You can cut a piece of stem in spring and plant it to get a new fuchsia. Whenever seed pods appear, nip them off; this helps more flowers to come. Give water in the summer.

It likes some shade and some sun, and plenty of air.

LOBELIA *Lobelia*

This one was named after James I's doctor, L'Obel. It has little blue flowers which grow in masses. Ask for a variety that trails downwards. It usually lasts one season only. Give plenty of water.

It likes light and air, and flowers best in a sunny place.

NOTE: Other annuals (sometimes called 'bedding' plants), which need the same conditions as lobelia and are suitable for baskets include: dwarf sweet peas, petunias, verbena, pendulous begonias, dwarf nasturtiums, mesembryanthemum, marigolds, alyssum, ageratum, toad flax, pansies, and many more. They cost only a few pence in early summer.

PERIWINKLE *Vinca minor*

This has evergreen leaves on trailing stems and blue flowers which last all through the summer. Roots appear at the tips of the stems: cut a bit off and plant in spring to make a new periwinkle. It doesn't mind too much about how much water it gets.

It likes a fairly shady position.

How to remove a plant from a pot

You may want to take a plant out of its pot in order to put it in a container with several others. Or it may be getting too big for the original pot and need transferring to a larger one. You can tell whether it is too big by looking to see whether the roots are beginning to grow through the hole at the bottom. Another sign is when the plant continually needs watering, or ceases to grow bigger – this means it hasn't enough soil for its needs.

Put your left hand over the top of the pot, with the stem held between your fingers.

Turn the pot upside down.

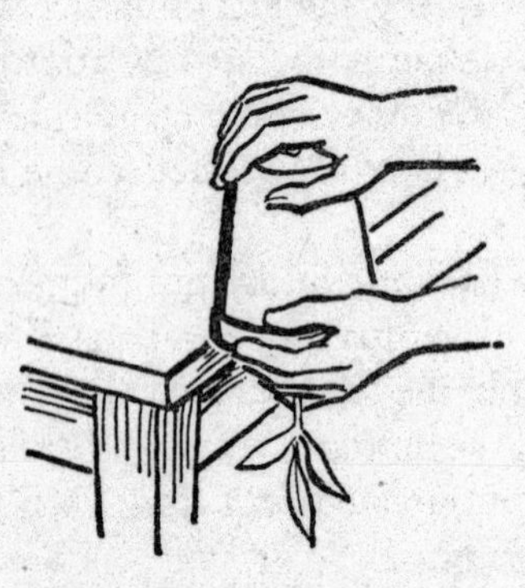

Tap it lightly on a table edge, to loosen the soil from the pot.

A slight shake, and the soil should come out of the pot in one lump, ready to plant or to put in a larger pot with more compost round it.

No 6 Desert Gardens

Cacti can be as big as trees, though not outdoors in this country, (you can see them at Kew and some other botanical gardens with greenhouses), but fortunately they grow very slowly and it is easy to make a little indoor garden with them. Needless to say, they like a warm spot to live in with lots of light and sun (like a windowsill in summer), as in the tropical deserts from which they come; but they will put up with a lot of neglect, even cold, as long as they are not in a damp atmosphere. They enjoy a spell outdoors in summer, and will flourish in a dry room with central heating, which many other plants hate.

Instead of having them in individual pots, you can create a tiny desert in any wide, shallow container such as a dish, an old baking-tin or a foil-lined box lid, about 3 inches deep. Tin can be painted with enamel or covered with self-adhesive plastic like Fablon or Con-tact. If you like, you can cover the soil with sand, and add some rocks and a snake of varnished clay or plasticine.

You can buy cacti ready-grown in pots quite cheaply, but they are easy to raise from seed in spring and early summer. Buy a packet of mixed cactus seed and wait with bated breath to see just what will show up months later: they come up at different times. As the drawings on pages 56–7 show, cacti come in a great variety of shapes.

Take a box with holes in the bottom; fill it with John Innes Compost No 1, into which you have mixed an equal quantity of coarse, washed sand, and sprinkle the seeds evenly all over it. Cover them with a little more of the mixture, very lightly water, and keep them in a warm room covered with foil (turn this daily).

When seedlings are ½–1 inch high, lift them out with a tiny spoon or fork and plant them 4 inches apart in the dish that is to be their final home, having first filled it with sand and compost over a $\frac{1}{2}$-inch layer of pebbles. If your mother has some tweezers, they help when handling prickly cacti, but be careful not to pinch the stem. Lightly water the compost.

Some cacti produce babies – little offshoots which can be cut off and then reared in the same way as seedlings. So keep an eye on friends' cacti to spot whether they have any offshoots ready

for adoption in this way. Or, in the case of others, a small tip can be cut off, left lying till the cut surface has hardened (about 2–3 days), and then grown like the seedlings.

Although cacti are desert plants, they need watering – but not too much: quite a lot, every 3–4 days, in summer; very little, every 3–4 weeks, in winter. Those that flower in winter need more water then. Add a little fertilizer once a fortnight in summer, or (in the case of Christmas cactus) when buds appear.

How do they survive in the dry desert? Mainly by storing

water in their flesh when the rainy season comes, from dew, and from water running deep underground.

Cacti do have flowers, but in some cases you may have to wait five years or more for them to happen! However, the ones on pages 56–7 should flower every year.

Growing cacti is so easy that you might make a profitable hobby out of selling them and thus provide yourself with funds for more gardening enterprises. They make good Christmas presents, or things to sell at charity shops and bazaars.

GYMNOCALYCIUM
The name means naked bud. Fleshy, ribbed cacti in a variety of shapes, with clumps of sharp spines. Usually just one or two quite big flowers on top – white, red or yellow.

MAMMILARIA
This name is Latin for 'nipples'. Dumpy little cacti covered in a fuzz of prickles. A ring of tiny flowers, usually red, should appear round the top once a year.

NOTOCACTUS
The southern cactus. This is another rounded one, covered with a fuzz of fine prickles. One or more yellow flowers with red outsides or centres may appear on top. Do not water in winter.

OPUNTIA
All sorts of shapes and sizes from little lumps to tree-like plants. A specially easy one to grow. Flowers are usually red, yellow or orange; some have very few prickles and others many.

REBUTIA
Rather like mammilaria but the flowers (of many colours) are larger and come from the sides of the cactus. It usually grows in clumps.

ZYGOCACTUS
Quite different in shape from the others, it is called Christmas cactus because its arching stems produce lots of red flowers in winter. Give it more water than most cacti, adding a little liquid fertilizer when the buds appear.

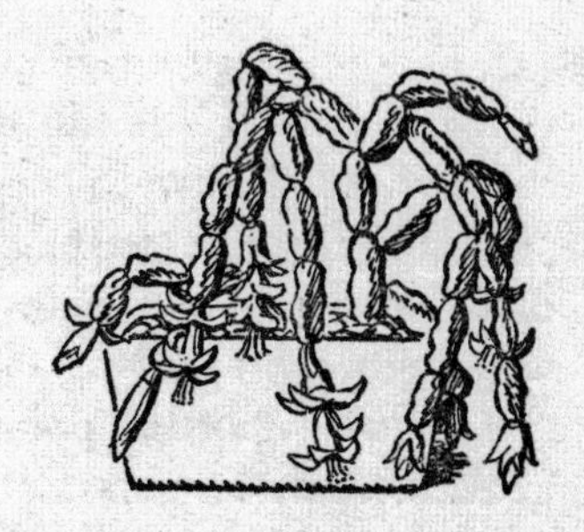

No 7 *Mini-Gardens*

Here's a way to have a whole garden of your own even if you've almost no space. Start in spring or early summer.

You can make a miniature garden – either an indoor or an outdoor one – provided you choose a mixture of plants (all of them small ones) with similar likes and dislikes to go in the same container. You should decide at the start whether the garden will go in a sunny or a shady place, warm or cool, and select only plants that like these conditions.

It is also better to have in one container only plants that have the same watering needs. If you do try to mix dry and damp types, you will have to keep one sort separate from the other – you can put those needing least water in their own little pots buried under the compost, and give them less water without affecting the others.

Another important point to remember is that some plants grow more than others, and these are better avoided if you don't want the miniatures to be lost in a jungle by the end of summer.

Always put the smallest plants at the front or side edges, and try to get a mixture of leaf shapes and colours for variety. Small creeping plants can trail over the edges.

To start your miniature garden you need a container only a few inches deep. For a very small garden indeed this could be a big soup-plate, an old baking-tin, the lid of a box (foil-lined) or a foil pie-dish. Garden shops sell long, shallow plastic trays, intended to stand flowerpots in, and these could be used for mini-gardens. For the tiniest garden ever, you could plant one or two things in a well-washed sea shell.

For a larger one, use something like an old washing-up bowl or see what the greengrocer can let you have. Shallow wood

fruit-boxes (3–4 inches deep, and lined with cooking foil if they have lots of slits) will do, but even better are the white polystyrene (plastic) ones in which some fruits are now delivered. Sometimes a builder has an old sink to get rid of.

What about drainage? Unless the container is made of porous material or has holes in it, perhaps you can pierce some, then cover loosely with bottle-tops as on page 112. If not, then the first need is to put in a $\frac{1}{2}$-inch layer of pebbles or charcoal as described on pages 34–5, to absorb any puddle of water that might otherwise collect in the bottom. Remember, with an indoor garden, that you will need something under it to protect furniture, if it has drainage holes.

Then put the compost in (John Innes No 1, or No 2 for permanent plants) to about $\frac{1}{2}$ inch from the top. Water well before you put any plants or cuttings in. You can top it, after putting the plants in, with a thin layer of gravel (which builders sell) if you like: not only for a neat look, but to slow down evaporation of moisture from the compost, and to keep mud off the plants.

For small plants and tiny bulbs you can dig holes with an old spoon; for cuttings, use your finger. If you have bought plants in pots and their ball of soil is deeper than your garden, gently shake the soil off the roots and spread them out sideways. Never crush them in. Press compost firmly down all round. Spray water daily over the plants (using a clean plastic squeezy bottle). If some plants later smother others, dig them up with a fork in spring or autumn, shake the soil off, and divide them up into pieces, each consisting of a stem and some roots. Replant one piece and put the others in pots or another garden, cutting their leaves and stems back to the size you want.

Outdoor gardens generally need frequent watering in dry weather. The soil may shrink away from the sides, in which case gently fork it over to fill the gap. On a really blazing day, put a piece of newspaper over the top from mid-morning to mid-afternoon. Remove weeds with a little fork or tweezers before they have a chance to spread or shed seeds. Water early or late in the day, never when the sun is full out: its rays shining through the water-drops might scorch the leaves.

Indoor gardens should be kept near the window and put outdoors, if possible, for a holiday during the summer. If the room is very dry, spray the leaves as well as watering the soil. Putting a transparent cover over for part of the time also helps to conserve moisture; on a small dish-garden you might use a plastic food-cover, or you can buy transparent plastic domes at some garden shops.

A miniature garden may be just a group of plants, as on page 58. Or you may think it will look prettier if it is laid out like a real garden and has more than just plants in it. Here is a list of ideas:

Pebbles with interesting colours and shapes (washed);
Little rocks, from seaside or hills (washed);
Little gnarled twigs, roots, and fircones;
Sand for paths, or tiny chips, sold for fishtanks;
Sea or snail shells (washed);
Tiny mosaic squares, for a patio or path (join them underneath with sticky insulating-tape);
Small toy animals, etc; toy farm fencing;
Fragment of mirror or foil, for a pool, or fill a little pot with water;
Small candle or nightlight, set well away from plants;
Arch made from wire to train a creeper over, or train it up a twig;
Urns, bridge, windmill, etc, made yourself from clay or Plasticine.

You can even make your own small indoor container from clay, as well as making ornaments for the garden. Roll a lump out on a cloth like pastry, ½ inch thick, and shape it into a dish or bowl about 2″ deep and 4–5″ across. Make a drainage hole in the bottom. To keep the clay from being softened by damp earth, wait several days for it to dry (don't put it near heat: this would crack it) and then brush the interior and all round the bottom of the hole with polyurethane varnish. If you want to colour the clay, use poster paint before varnishing. Clay and some other modelling materials dry hard (and can be painted); Plasticine does not, so use it for ornaments, not containers.

To make your own outdoor container, you could simply arrange about ten bricks in a rectangular border and fill the middle with compost.

On pages 68–77 are suggestions for plants you will find suitable for small gardens. In addition, you could select from other plants and bulbs described in this book, picking the smallest ones only.

There is one category of plants particularly suited to minigardens, provided they can be put in a warm and sunny spot, indoors or out. Unlike many other plants, lots of them like central heating. They are the succulents.

Succulents include cacti (*see* Chapter 6) and also two other large families, the sempervivums (which means 'living forever') and the sedums, which come in a great variety of forms. Some like indoors, and some must go out. All have fleshy leaves, sometimes pink as well as green, and some have tiny flowers of differing colours. You could create a delightful miniature rock garden with these, for they tend to spread and creep about, half-covering the stones, rather like cushions. They don't need a lot of watering and can safely be left uncared for when you go on holiday. Many will even grow on a bare windowsill or wall without compost! Because these plants are such spreaders, most friends who have any will gladly give you cuttings which will soon multiply in your mini-garden. If you want to mix them in with plants that need more watering, make little hillocks to plant them in – that way, water will drain away from them.

If you feel like collecting, and perhaps even becoming an expert on one particular kind of plant, succulents could be a very good group to choose, provided you have the warm and sunny conditions needed. There are hundreds of varieties to collect, but they need little space.

There is a very wide range of plants called alpines, some of which are lovely for growing in little gardens. Though they live for years, they always stay small (*see* pages 68–9). Little trees and alpine plants are sold by specialist plant shops; look under 'nurserymen' in the yellow pages of the phone book to find the ones in your area, or buy them by post from the addresses at the end of the chapter.

Many of the smaller pot plants and bulbs written about in other chapters can also be used. It is best to keep them in their individual pots, arranging stones, moss, etc, around them, with some higher than others to give a banked effect. You could buy tiny annuals for a temporary garden, but remember they will flower only once, and be sure to ask for dwarf varieties. Suitable ones include alyssum, arabis, marigolds, nemesia and verbena.

Whether indoors or out, most of the plants need fertilizer every month, especially during summer, and this is best added to the water you give them (*see* page 28). You should also keep an eye open for insect pests, or diseases that attack the leaves (*see* pages 136–7).

And what about growing a weed garden? For a start, what exactly *are* weeds anyway? Someone has defined them as any plants growing where you don't want them to be. A farmer might regard a superb rose as a weed if he found it slap in the middle of his cabbage field.

Some of the plants that gardeners tear up and throw away are beautiful to look at. Think of the brilliant colour of the dandelion, the fascinating jagged leaves that give it its name (dens-de-lion – teeth of the lion), the pretty puff of thistledown that succeeds the flower – but don't let this blow about and spread seeds onto other people's gardens.

Carefully dig up a selection of small weeds in spring (don't break the roots) and plant them in a container, arranging and caring for them in the same way as other plants. Thin them out often, for most weeds spread rapidly.

Here is a list of some which are small and pretty and should transplant well into a miniature garden to keep outdoors:

Speedwell: a creeping plant with blue flowers, 1–2 inches high. *Daisy:* rosette of leaves with white-pink flowers, 2–3 inches. *Scarlet pimpernel:* creeping plant with red flowers, 1–2 inches (the flowers close up when rain is coming). *Lady's bedstraw:* tiny yellow flowers, 1–2 inches high. And lots more – borrow a wildflower book from the library and go hunting. Most like sun or light shade. Keep watering them after you have transplanted them, and whenever the weather is hot.

Most gardens have a tree or two, and the mini-garden need be no exception provided it stands in a sheltered position outdoors, away from wind. Real trees can be persuaded to grow as dwarf versions of themselves, some as small as 6 inches, though patience is needed. The Japanese are experts at this, and they call their art Bonsai (which means 'plant in a pot'). Some Bonsai trees live to be as much as 500 years old, but these are rare, and very costly.

You can make a little Bonsai tree yourself from a seed planted in autumn in a pot outdoors and left till spring (such as an acorn from an oak tree, a beech nut, or a cherry stone); or – needing less patience! – from a tiny seedling found growing in the countryside one spring.

If you dig up a seedling, be very careful not to break the roots;

and keep it wrapped in a damp cloth until you get home, when it should be planted at once. Put it in damp compost, and spray it with water daily for weeks to come. The shallower the pot, the more often will water be needed – daily, except in winter. You can add a little fertilizer (*see* page 28) to the water during summer.

Acorns and other tree seeds should be left in pots outdoors to grow. When they are a few inches high, they can be put into bigger pots containing John Innes Compost No 2 – one seedling per pot.

In order to stop a naturally large-growing tree reaching its full size, most of the new leaf-buds have to be cut off as soon as they appear. At first you need to leave any that are growing at the sides, but nip off those at the top as soon as they appear; check each day. After the first year, you will probably need to remove side as well as top buds in order to keep the tree small. And if any branches look weak or straggly, they should be cut off completely, in spring or autumn.

You also need to trim the roots, if you can. If you intend to do

this, the little tree must not be placed in among other plants but grown in its own tiny pot, which can be lifted out for the purpose. This could be a cream pot with lots of holes pierced low in the sides with a hot skewer. After a year or so, the roots will start pushing through the sides, and this is when to cut them off.

Now for the real secret of Bonsai – how to make not just the tree but also the leaves extra small. In June, cut all the leaves off one by one – but be sure not to cut their stalks right off because there is a tiny bud at the bottom of each one. From these buds, new and smaller leaves will come.

An easy alternative to growing a miniature tree is simply to put a leafy twig in. It will last quite a long time, and can be renewed. Evergreens (which do not shed their leaves in winter) are particularly useful, especially fir trees.

There are also some trees and shrubs that are naturally low, some as little as 6–12 inches. They cost more to buy, but do not need the special Bonsai care (*see* pages 65–6).

If you want to create a little lawn among your miniature plants and trees, sow grass seed (ask for the very finest quality) and keep it 'mowed' with nail-scissors. Or plant moss, thyme or camomile to make a herb 'carpet'.

Once you become a real enthusiast for mini-gardening, send for a catalogue of hundreds of special tiny plants to Miniature Gardens Ltd, Chignal Smealey, Chelmsford, Essex, and buy a copy of Anne Ashberry's book, *Gardens in Miniature* (40p) from them. If you live in the north, get a catalogue from R. E. Allenby, Garden Flats Lane, Donnington, Yorks.

Some small plants for indoors

Be sure to get the right varieties: others may be huge! The first three are small enough for soup-plate gardens.

AUSTRALIAN VIOLET *Viola hederacea*
This little violet, 2 inches high, has white flowers with purple splashes from May to October, and ivy-shaped leaves.
It likes a cool, but not cold, place with moderate sun.

BABY'S TEARS *Helxine soleirolii aurea*
Tiny, golden, permanent leaves on creeping stems spread until a 'carpet' is formed. It will brim over the edges of the container. Don't give it much water.
It likes either sun or shade.

CENTAURY *Centaurium portense* or *scilloides*
Its brilliant pink flowers, 2–3 inches high, last all summer, and it has glossy leaves and climbing stems.
It likes lots of sun, and well-drained soil.

CRASSULA *Crassula bolusii* (or *cooperi*)
Another very tiny one, which has a rosette of evergreen leaves, pale green above and dark red below, and clusters of pink flowers in summer and autumn. Give it little water.

It likes light, but not too much heat.

PIMPERNEL *Anagallis collina*
Flame-coloured flowers throughout summer on a very low-growing plant, which will overhang the sides of the container if you plant it at the edge. (Its cousin, *A. tenella*, has pink bell-like flowers.)

It likes lots of sunshine. (A. *tenella* prefers shade and moist ground.)

DWARF HINOKI CYPRESS
Chamaecyparis obtusa nana

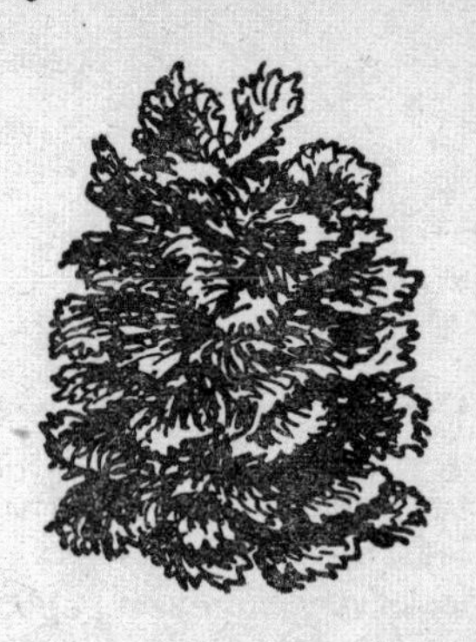

A little clumpy, spreading tree, no more than a foot high, with dark-green, mossy, evergreen leaves on fan-like branches. It needs a fair amount of water at all times.

It likes light but not too much heat. Never put near gas or coal fires, as it doesn't like fumes.

DWARF HINOKI CYPRESS
(another sort)
Chamaecyparis obtusa sanderi (ericoides)

A little upright tree, with blue-green evergreen leaves, sometimes turning bronze in autumn. Water well.

It likes light, but not heat or fumes.

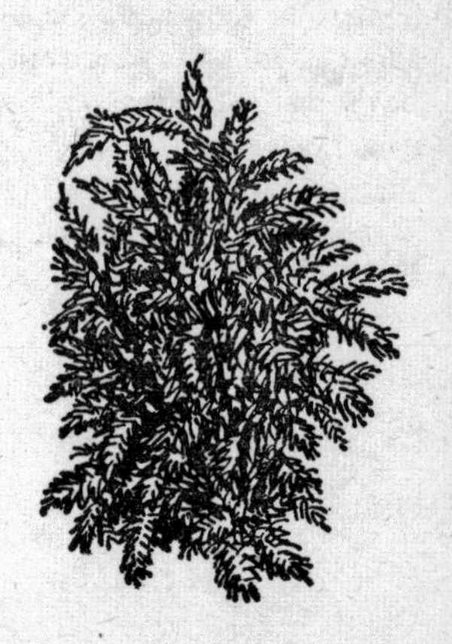

DWARF CYPRESS *Chamaecyparis pisifera squarrosa intermedia*

The smaller the plant, the longer the name, it seems! An even lower, round, and very dense bush with silver-blue evergreen feathery leaves on drooping branches. If it gets straggly, trim it with scissors. Water well.

It likes light but not heat or fumes.

DWARF JUNIPER — *Juniperus squamata wilsonii*

Grey-green leaves (evergreen) on reddish branches which curve downwards. It looks very effective if put beside a little pool like a weeping willow. Sprinkle a little garden lime on in spring (*see* page 80) and water well.

It likes light, but not heat or fumes.

MINIATURE ROSE BUSH — *Rosa*

For much less than the trees, you can now buy little rose plants only a few inches high (though unless you keep trimming them they will grow to 6–10 inches). The flowers, in various colours, will be only about ½ inch big. A miniature rose can be grown outdoors as well as in: in fact, even indoor ones like a spell outdoors in summer. Water well.

It likes sunshine, fresh air – and not a hot dry room.

ASPERULA *Asperula* (miniature varieties)

A very low-growing plant with white or pink flowers in summer, and rough-textured leaves (*asper* is Latin for rough).

It likes sunshine, but will manage in shade.

CINQUEFOIL *Potentilla nitida*

Pink, red or white flowers show up in summer against the silvery leaves, 2–4 inches high.

It likes a dry sunny spot.

SAXIFRAGE (ROCKFOIL)

Saxifraga – miniature cushion (*kabschia*) varieties

Most kabschia saxifrages have silvery-green leaves and make little cushions from which in spring delicate flowers arise (white, pink or yellow), sometimes on red stems.

It likes sunshine and well-drained soil: add sand to the compost.

THRIFT *Armeria caespitosa*

Only an inch high, with puffball heads of pink flowers in early summer.

It likes sun and well-drained soil – add sand to the compost.

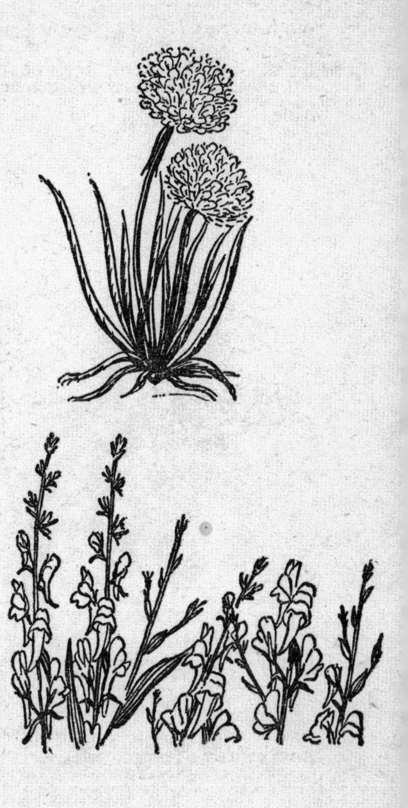

TOADFLAX *Linaria alpina*

Like a tiny, compact-growing snapdragon, with violet, white or pink flowers (some with orange lips) in summer. Give it a sprinkling of garden lime in spring (*see* page 80).

It likes lots of sunshine, and sand added to the compost.

Some mini-trees and shrubs for outdoors

BARBERRY — *Berberis darwinii corallina compacta*

Dark evergreen leaves, sharp prickles and orange-yellow flowers in spring. Under 9 inches high. It sometimes produces little red fruits (don't eat them). Don't give it too much water.

It likes either sun or shade.

BLACK SPRUCE — *Picea mariana nana*

The blue-green 'needles' are fragrant, and in spring they are red-tipped. The little globe-like tree has branches like a Christmas tree, under 4 inches high to start with, and never more than a foot high.

It likes moist compost, some sun, shelter from wind and clean air.

DWARF JAPANESE CEDAR — *Cryptomeria japonica vilmoriniana*

A quaint tree with masses of light-green permanent leaves that turn bronze in winter, 6–12 inches high.

It likes moist compost, some sun, shelter from wind and clean air.

JASMINE *Jasminum parkeri*

This has scented, bright yellow flowers in summer and is usually under 10 inches high. Its stiff little branches bear tiny glossy evergreen leaves, and shiny black seeds in autumn.

It likes sunshine and a well-drained compost.

DWARF WILLOW *Salix reticulata*

A very low-growing, round-leaved shrub, 5–6 inches high – not at all like the familiar weeping willow. It has reddish catkins in early summer and shiny brown shoots. It sheds its leaves in winter. Add peat to the compost, and give it plenty of water.

It likes a sunny place and well-drained compost.

HOUSELEEK *Sempervivum arachnoideum*
An evergreen rosette of small, round, green leaves covered with a white 'cobweb' all the year (*arachne* is Greek for spider). Its flowers are star-shaped and pink-red in summer. Three inches high.

It likes sunshine, and stones in the compost.

MOUNTAIN HOUSELEEK
Sempervivum montanum
Small rosettes of fleshy, dark-green leaves and purple-pink flowers in summer. Two inches high. It spreads by producing baby plants. Give it a little water.

It likes lots of sunshine.

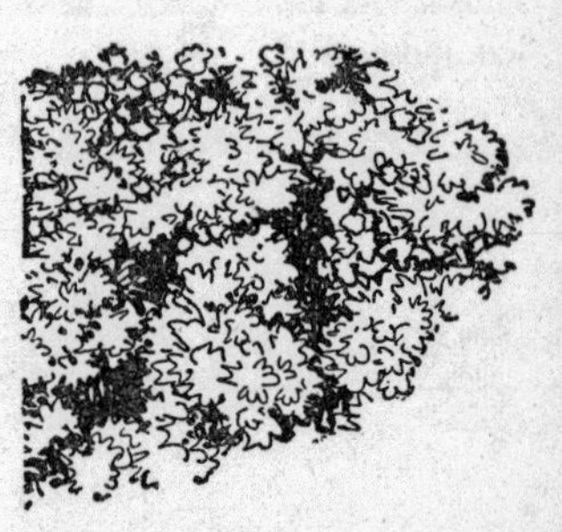

POWDERY STONECROP *Sedum spathulifolium cappa blanca*
The grey-green rosettes of leaves look as though they had been sprinkled with white powder. Yellow flowers in summer. Three inches high. Give only a little water.

It likes lots of sunshine, and stones in the compost.

PURPLE STONECROP *Sedum spathulifolium purpureum*

The rosettes of leaves are nearly white when young but turn purple-red and are lovely all the year. Four inches high. Yellow flowers in early summer. Give little water.

It likes lots of sunshine, and stones in the compost.

WALL PEPPER STONECROP *Sedum acre*

A creeping little plant under 2 inches high which forms a mat of shiny evergreen leaves. Yellow flowers in summer. It will trail over the edges of a container.

It likes sunshine and well-drained compost.

QUESTION TIME No 3

What do plants live on?

Plants take in some of their nourishment through their leaves, and some through their roots.

The leaves get carbon dioxide and oxygen from the air, and energy from the sun and light to stimulate the making and digestion of the foods they need. The roots absorb lots of minerals (particularly nitrogen, phosphates and potash) from the soil, from water or from fertilizers. Both leaves and roots drink in moisture.

So you see how important it is to put plants in a spot with all the air, light and warmth they require; and to give them as much water as they want (preferably clear rain water) and fertilizer, if in pots. If you don't, you will starve them to death.

What is compost?

A good soil for pot plants specially mixed in certain proportions with sand and peat and fertilizers so as to give the correct texture the roots need at different stages and the right amount of food initially. The best formulae were worked out by the John Innes Horticultural Institution, so these are called John Innes Composts and, as plants have different requirements, the bags are labelled '1', '2' or '3' – '3' being the richest.

Why not dig up garden soil to use?

Some garden soil is good, but in many places it is poor. And as a pot holds very little soil, all of it must be really nourishing, of the right texture and ingredients, and without weed-seeds and pests.

Why are bulbs planted in bulb fibre?

Most don't need compost because there is plenty of nourishment in the bulb itself to produce flowers the first time. The

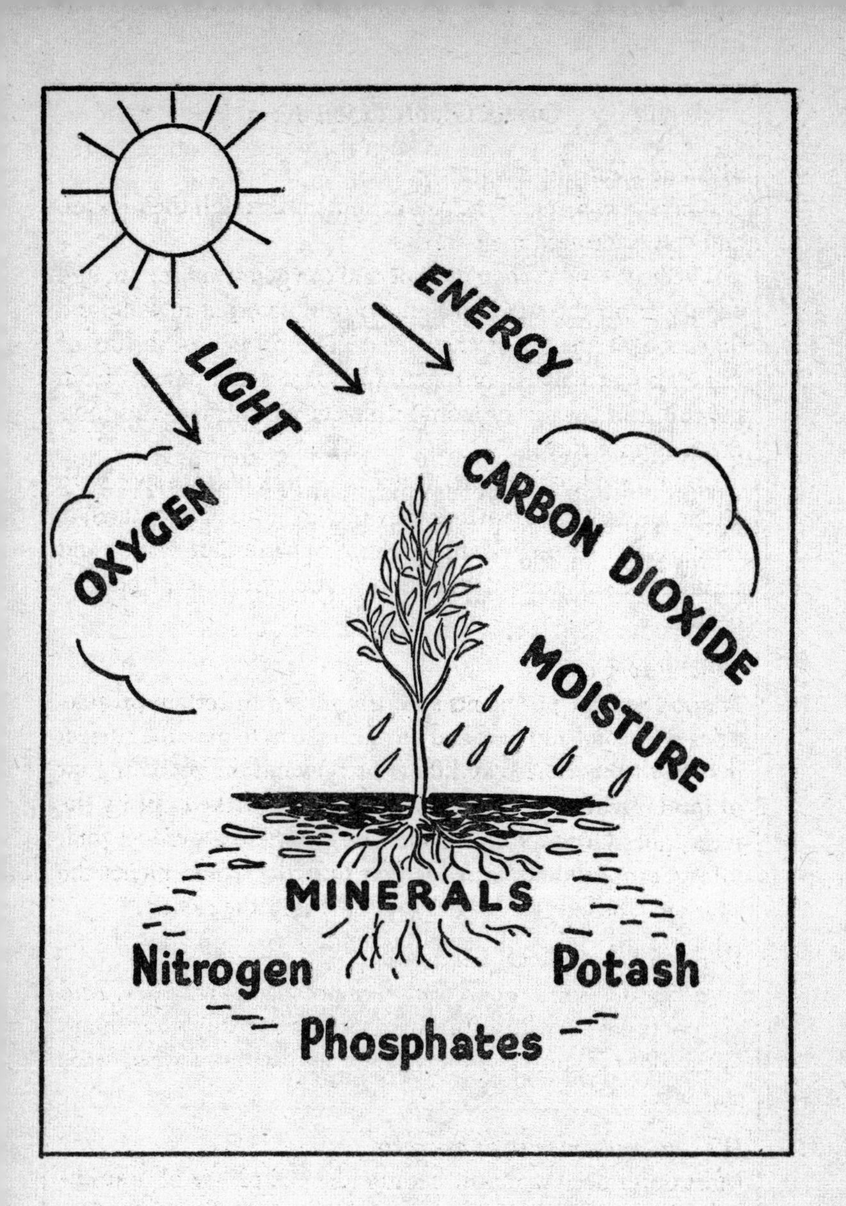
ENERGY
LIGHT
OXYGEN
CARBON DIOXIDE
MOISTURE
MINERALS
Nitrogen
Potash
Phosphates

fibre's purpose is just to support the bulb, and hold the moisture it needs. If you want to keep the bulbs for other years, then you must add fertilizer to them after flowering until the leaves die down. This is so that they can build up their natural bulb 'larder' again.

What are sand and peat sometimes added for?

There is no nourishment in sand, but it stops the compost getting caked – so water drains away more easily. Plants that particularly dislike sogginess benefit from sand in the compost. Peat has very few minerals in it, but it is often used on top of compost simply to prevent the moisture in it from evaporating – important to plants that like moist soil. It helps to improve the condition of the soil by making it more crumbly, and both aids water drainage and yet retains moisture like a sponge if need be. It also helps to make chalky soils (which are alkaline) better for most plants – peat is rather acid.

What are fertilizers?

They are minerals (or mixtures of minerals) to make soil or composts richer – especially useful when a plant is growing fast (usually spring or summer), or in a pot with only a limited amount of compost on which to feed. In this book, three kinds are recommended – liquid or granular ones which contain a general, well-balanced mixture of minerals; bone meal (ground-up animal-bones), which gives phosphates – very good for roots; and lime (preferably hydrated lime), which supplies calcium to plants that need it and generally helps to keep the soil in good condition.

No 8 *Bulbs, Tubers, Corms and Rhizomes*

(*see* page 92 for the differences between these four)

Bulbs can be grown indoors or out, but ask when you buy to make sure you get the kind you want.

Autumn is the time when most of them should be planted (exceptions to this are described later) and they will then flower in spring. If you want bulbs that flower earlier, indoors, look in the shops during August and September for bulbs labelled to say that they have been specially treated so that they will bloom by Christmas. There are also other bulbs to flower indoors during January and February.

Indoors

The usual way is to take a plastic or china bowl (without a drainage hole) and buy a bag of bulb-fibre to fill it to about an inch from the top. Bulb fibre is a mixture of peat, crushed shells and absorbent charcoal which holds moisture well but supplies little nourishment – the bulb itself contains all that is needed. Wet the fibre well before you plant the bulbs. All except crocuses (which should be planted ½ inch deep) should have their tips just above the surface, with a little space between each of them and the edge of the bowl. Don't mix different kinds of bulbs, because some grow at different speeds from others.

Now put the bowl in a cool and airy place – in the dark, or else lightly covered with paper or dark plastic to keep the light out. Leave it for 2–3 months, occasionally adding water if the fibre dries. When the leaves are 1–3 inches high and you can see the beginnings of the flower buds between them, bring the bowl into the light; a few days after that transfer it into a warm room – but don't put it near a fire or in a draught. From now on the bulbs will need more water (be sure not to pour it on the buds) with a few drops of liquid fertilizer in it.

In about three weeks time, they should be in flower. After flowering has finished, you can either plant the bulbs in the garden in spring, or you can stand the bowls outside. Add fertilizer when watering, and when the leaves have shrivelled away tip the bulbs out and store them in a cool, dry place before planting again in the autumn. But next year the flowers may be smaller.

You can also grow bulbs in water (*see* Chapter 2).

Of the garden bulbs shown on pages 85–91, some varieties of the following can also be grown indoors:

crocus	daffodil
narcissus	glory of the snow
grape hyacinth	hyacinth
squill	tulip
snowdrop	iris reticulata
colchicum	lily
	montbretia

Outdoors

Bulbs outdoors can be planted in pots of John Innes Compost No 2 or in garden soil. If they are in pots these should have some broken 'crocks' (bits of broken pots, or pebbles) put over the drainage holes at the bottom; or, if there are no holes, an inch of charcoal should go in before the compost. Tall ones, like lilies, need big pots.

The bulbs should be buried 2–6 inches down: the bigger the bulb the deeper it should be. Water the hole before putting the bulb in. And be sure no stones go on top when you cover it with soil.

Little bulbs should be only an inch apart and are better in clusters rather than rows. Others should be 2–6 inches apart, depending on how big the plant will grow. Some of the big lilies should be a foot apart. Little bulbs go at the front of a border, big ones farther back.

Most bulbs stay in the soil year after year, and some will multiply and spread of their own accord. If a clump gets very crowded, you can dig it up gently and separate the group of little bulbs you will then find, in order to start several new groups.

Exceptions to this are tulips, gladioli and dahlias. When they have finished flowering and their leaves have turned yellow, dig their bulbs up, cut off the leaves and put the bulbs in a cool, dry place until it is time to plant them again. If you have very dry soil with a lot of sun you can leave them in, with a cover of dry leaves or peat on top each winter.

Some other bulbs are sensitive to frost. Hyacinths and some lilies, for instance, may not survive the winter unless they are protected by a thick layer of leaves or peat or ashes before the very cold weather starts. In fact, in very cold winters, all bulbs benefit from protection of this kind.

Most bulbs like moisture in the soil, so keep watering them

when it is dry in spring and summer until the leaves die, but not so much that they get soggy. Choose a place where rain-water runs away freely. You could help matters by putting a handful of sand at the bottom of each hole before you plant the bulbs, as this helps water drain away.

If your garden soil is sticky and heavy with clay or chalk, mix some sand or peat in with it before putting bulbs in, and at the same time add some powdery bone-meal fertilizer.

Bulbs like fertilizer. The best way to give it to them is to scatter Growmore granules on the soil round the leaves of the plant before flowers appear and after they have finished; or to use liquid fertilizer when watering. Dry fertilizers need forking into the soil a little, but don't disturb the roots.

You may think the leaves left after flowering has finished look a bit untidy, but don't cut them off until they have turned yellow. For months, the leaves will be absorbing natural foods from the air, rain and sunshine and feeding them to the bulbs below, which will then use them to produce flowers next year.

Most are for planting, tip uppermost, in the autumn. Ones to plant in spring are meadow saffron, autumn-flowering crocuses, ranunculus, some anemones, some irises, montbretia, lilies, dahlias and gladioli.

ACONITE *Eranthis hyemalis*

This has little yellow flowers like buttercups early in spring, surrounded by pretty ruffs of leaves. It will spread of its own accord.

It likes a moist, shady spot and not too much peat.

ANEMONE *Anemone*

Most varieties flower in spring, but some are later, and you can plant them in either autumn or spring. The flowers are of mixed colours – red, purple, pink, white. It is sometimes difficult to see which way up to plant the corm (bulb) – in which case plant it sideways.

It likes a little sunshine, or light shade; a good deal of moisture.

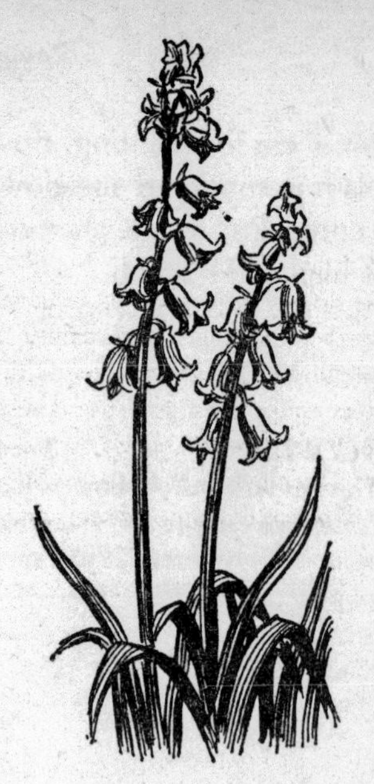

BLUEBELL *Endymion*

This grows happily under trees and bushes and spreads easily. The plants have stems of lovely blue flowers in spring, and sometimes you can also get pink or white ones.

It likes a moist, shady spot.

CROCUS *Crocus*

See Chapter 2. Plant spring-flowering ones in autumn and autumn-flowering ones in spring. Like all small corms, it can be planted in grass under a tree provided that the lawn mower isn't used there while it is growing; or in the cracks between paving stones.

It likes a sunny position and well-drained soil.

CYCLAMEN *Cyclamen*

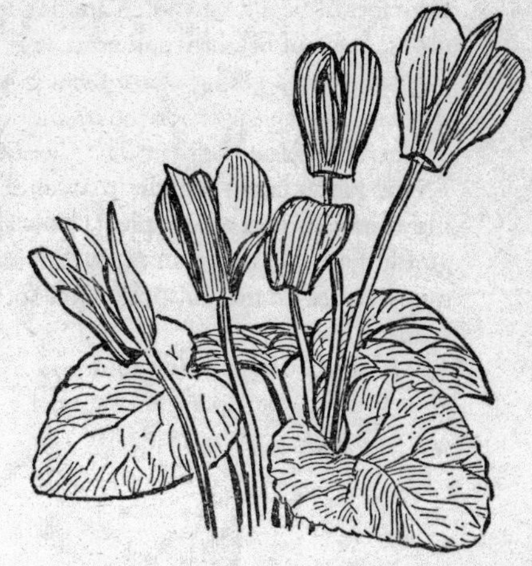

Some flower in August, some in autumn, some even in winter, with dainty, pinkish-purple flowers. It grows splendidly in clusters under trees, and spreads itself happily if given some peat or leaf-mould on top each autumn. *See also* Chapter 3.

It likes some shade and well-drained soil.

DAFFODIL (*NARCISSUS*) *Narcissus*

The same plant, but daffodils have big trumpets. In many sizes, mostly yellow or white, some fragrant. It flowers in spring. If a clump gets crowded, divide it in two in July.

It likes some sunshine and well-drained soil.

DAHLIA *Dahlia*

Some have simple, daisy-like flowers, some have lots of petals, and some are like spiky mops: big and brightly coloured. It is easiest to buy a young plant, then, in the autumn, dig up the tuber (bulb) and store it till spring. You then cut the tuber into several pieces, and put each in a pot of moist peat to start a new plant, which can go out into the garden in May. Tall sorts may need to be tied to sticks. Give lots of fertilizer in summer.

It likes to be kept inside till frosts are past, and then put in a sunny spot.

GLADIOLUS *Gladiolus*

This is usually tall and stiff, with showy flowers (red, pink, yellow, orange, white) in summer, and leaves like sword-blades – the name is Latin for 'little sword'. Plant it in spring in a hole with some sand at the bottom, and cover with 2 inches of peat or ashes in winter (in the north, it is better to dig it up). Tall ones may need to be tied to sticks. Give fertilizer in summer.

It likes plenty of sunshine.

GLORY OF THE SNOW
Chionodoxa luciliae

Starry blue flowers with white centres appear in clusters very early in the year and have shiny, strap-like leaves. This little plant likes to be dug up and separated when it multiplies, because it gets too crowded.

It likes a fairly sunny spot.

RAPE HYACINTH *Muscari*

ı spring, this has bright blue flowers like
ny grapes on each stem, and thin leaves
ke grass. It quickly spreads and is easy
› grow.

It likes plenty of sun.

HYACINTH

ee Chapter 2.

IRIS *Iris*

There is an enormous number of kinds in all sorts of colours and sizes (even miniature ones), flowering at different times of the year. The flowers are very elaborate but the leaves are plain – like sword-blades. The bearded iris is the easiest one to grow: plant it in spring. The one for indoors is *Iris reticulata.*

It likes sunshine and a rather chalky soil.

ILY *Lilium*

erhaps the most beautiful flower there is.
Jsually very tall; many are scented, and
ıere is a huge choice of colours. Some
ave only 1–2 big trumpet-shaped flowers;
thers have clusters, with small slender
:aves growing up the stems. Plant in
›ring. You can find varieties which,
etween them, will flower all through
›ring and summer. Protect the plant in
/inter.

It likes some sunshine, and ground that
never soggy.

MEADOW SAFFRON *Colchicum*

Sometimes called Naked Boy because its pinky, crocus-shaped flower comes up in late summer or autumn on a tall stem without any leaves. The leaves follow in the spring. Plant it in August.

It likes a little sun.

MONTBRETIA *Montbretia*

Small orange-yellow flowers grow up a tall stem in autumn, with slender, grassy leaves. The corm (bulb) needs to be put in during March and will multiply fast.

It likes a warm spot and sunshine, sheltered from wind.

RANUNCULUS *Ranunculus*

The garden version of the ordinary buttercup. The flowers, on 9-inch stems, appear in May and June, in many colours. Plant in either October or March.

It likes lots of sun, and dislikes soggy or sticky soil.

SNOWDROP *Galanthus*

Delicate white bells appear very early in the year and hang in a row on each curving stem. The leaves are long and plain.

It likes cool, moist ground, either shady or with a little sun.

SQUILL *Scilla*

Early in spring, starry flowers (blue, pink or white) appear like small bluebells, with the leaves following later. It is related to glory of the snow.

It likes a moderate amount of sun.

TULIP *Tulipa*

All sorts of plain and multi-colours, in many sizes, flowering from February to May. In summer, dig the bulb up and store to replant in late October. If the garden is very warm and dry, it can be left in.

It likes plenty of sun.

QUESTION TIME No 4
WHAT IS A BULB?

A bulb is the fleshy part of a plant, growing mainly underground; the word is often used also to describe a particular kind of thick root. All types act as larders for the plants, because they store foods for them to live on as they grow.

Bulbs, proper, are fleshy-leaved shoots which produce the stem, leaves, roots and flowers of a plant each year. The leaves and roots feed new food back into the bulb before they

die; and the bulb stores this up ready for next year's growth. Examples: onions, tulips.

Tubers are swollen underground stems which produce buds (from which stems, flowers and leaves come) and roots. The roots make more tubers for next year. Examples: potatoes, dahlias.

Corms are also fleshy underground stems storing food for the roots, stems, leaves and flowers to feed on. Sometimes a baby corm appears alongside the old one, to make a new plant. Examples: crocus, gladiolus.

Rhizomes are creeping swollen stems sometimes half out of the soil, from which roots grow downwards, and stems with leaves and flowers upwards. Example: bearded irises.

No 9 Back Yards, Front Areas, Balconies

If you live in a town, especially in an old house, your only outdoor space may be hemmed in by walls, and with no soil – or such poor soil that nothing much will grow in it. Almost certainly your 'garden' gets very little sun – or maybe some bits get too much and become parched. It may also be too dry – or too damp. What can you possibly do with it? Or with a balcony?

To solve the problem of no soil, buy compost and put it in tubs, pots or boxes. Or turn back to the chapter on gardening without soil (Chapter 2).

To solve the problem of poor soil, dig into it as much peat, sand and fertilizer (such as Growmore) as you can, before planting anything.

To solve the problem of no sun, choose shade-loving plants. (Too much sun? Then look out for sun-loving ones.)

And as for those high walls, put them to good use by growing creepers up them, or fastening plant baskets to them (*see* Chapter 5). If you grow creepers on house walls, fix something like trellis or plastic-covered wire to them first so that the plants don't start rooting into the brickwork or making the walls damp. But, before you start, ask your parents' permission (and their help); they may or may not be delighted to have the backyard transformed!

Although you can buy plastic pots, troughs and window-boxes in all kinds of shapes and sizes, there are plenty of other containers that can be used. Here are some ideas:

old buckets and baths
wooden boxes and crates
barrels and bins
plastic packing-boxes and cases

old washing-up bowls
old sinks and tanks
big saucepans, wastepaper bins, lengths of drainpipe, foil-lined baskets (and even chamber-pots!)

If you use a container that has previously had some liquid in it, it must be thoroughly washed with suds and well rinsed. Never use oil containers: traces will kill plants. Plastic and pottery containers are durable, but metal or wood will eventually rust or rot (though not for years). Wood can be painted

with Cuprinol to give it longer life, but don't use creosote, which poisons plants. Cuprinol comes in various colours; after painting it on, let the box or tub air for a few days. For metal there are special anti-rust paints to put on before the ordinary paint. A light colour will improve the looks of the containers and make them match one another. Holes for drainage must be pierced in the bottom if none exist already, and stand the container on a few stones to give space for draining. To pierce holes in metal, hammer nails through. With china, use a drill and masonry-bit.

An earthenware sink, bath or basin could be given a 'natural', stone-like finish by painting the outside with black bitumastic paint (ordinary paint would flake off) and then, while the paint is still wet – and with your hand protected by an old glove – putting all over it sawdust or wood shavings mixed with soil.

This will give a rough texture on which moss and lichen will gradually grow of their own accord.

Before you start planting, it might be a good idea to whitewash the wall behind the plants (or, better still, use cement paint – white, pink or yellow) which will make a gloomy yard seem brighter and will show up the plants to advantage. If you are going to grow any climbing sorts of plants, you will need to fix onto the walls something which they can clamber up. This could be trellis (wood, or plastic-coated wire mesh) or, if they

have tendrils or stems that twist, just strings or wires. To fasten these on, ironmongers sell special big galvanized nails to hammer into walls. Or, for a naturalistic effect, you could 'plant' a tall, bare bough from a tree and grow a creeper up this. Another idea is to make a creeper-covered arch out of trellis which could stand against a wall and frame a pot, a statuette or a mural you had painted on the wall yourself with outdoor emulsion paints. Balcony railings are just the thing for climbers.

If you put a plant trough on a balcony, or on a window-ledge at the bottom of the house (never put one higher – it might fall off and hurt someone badly), put a few stones under so that water can drain away freely and not soak the balcony or window-sill.

If the backyard ground between your plant pots or beds doesn't look very nice, you might be able to get (free or very cheaply) broken paving-slabs from a builder's merchant, local council depot or a site that is being dismantled, if there is a family car to fetch them in. Lay them out and fill the gaps between them with well-washed sand bought from a builder's yard, mixed up with some peat from a garden shop. You can then poke some tiny plants between the slabs and they will grow. Or, if you bought a bag of ready-mix cement and spread this (you'll need help because it is so heavy), you could make a pattern in it with

pieces of broken china, pebbles and shells as a centre-piece in your yard. Or draw lines on it with a stick while still wet: you could imitate crazy-paving if you like.

The plants will need feeding with fertilizer. If you are watering them regularly, especially in summer, this could be a liquid fertilizer mixed into the water (*see* page 28). But if yours is a damp yard and you do not need to water them much, a dry fertilizer would be better – like Growmore. You just scatter this round plants once during spring, and lightly scratch it into the soil with a fork. In autumn, you do the same thing but this time use bone meal; and then put a layer of peat over the top.

Remember that big containers need a lot to fill them and will be heavy to move about. Put them where they are to stay, preferably on some bricks to allow for drainage and to discourage pests like woodlice from lurking underneath, then half fill them with old bricks and stones, leaving only a foot or so for compost (John Innes No 3 this time – the richest one of all); for a tree, you should leave room for more compost. All containers need stones, broken pottery, brick bits, etc, at the bottom to let water from the compost drain through freely.

An alternative to a garden of pots is one with a raised bed about 1–2 feet high, or more. For this you need to collect a lot of old bricks and broken slabs and pile them up in a row

1½–2 ft from a garden wall, sloping slightly backwards (don't ever pile them alongside the wall of a house, because this would make it damp). Then you empty a sack of compost behind them. Or you could make a circle or square of bricks (sloping slightly inwards) and pour the compost into the middle, stuffing some between the bricks too so that you can grow little creeping plants there. Because bricks and slabs contain lime, do not plant among them things that hate lime – heathers, azaleas, ceanothus, genista, for example. An old tyre, painted white, could provide a rim for such a flowerbed.

Instead of bricks you could buy a sack of peat blocks from a garden shop (but these cost more). Most plants like peat.

Be sure not to put your raised bed over a drain – you might block it.

And one more idea for gardening without a garden: lay a plastic bag of compost on the ground, cut a few criss-cross slits in the top and put flowering plants or tomatoes in. Make a few small holes at the bottom for drainage.

And yet another: make a circle of garden mesh (about 6 in high) joined with wire. Line it with plastic sheeting and fill with compost.

As for what to plant in the tubs and pots, you can use any from Chapters 5, 7 and 8, which have lists of plants and bulbs that can be used. Choose those that like sun or shade, wet or dry areas, according to the conditions you can give them. Some of your pot plants from indoors will like to spend a holiday in the garden and can be put outside in the summer. There are also lots of annual plants (which flower only during the first year) that you can buy very cheaply from Woolworth's, greengrocers' and garden nurseries, and they can make a lovely splash of colour in containers from about May to October. Don't forget, too, that some of the grasses, mosses and sedges found in the countryside can also be useful for planting between paving stones.

When planting any of the plants suggested, be careful to make the hole large enough not to cramp the roots, and the soil should come as far up the stem as it was originally when you bought them. Remember that the bigger the final size of the plant, the bigger the container or bed it will require.

On the next pages are described some plants that will flourish even if your yard has very little sun – and also a number of ferns which positively prefer shade.

ASTILBE *Astilbe*

This produces lovely upright sprays of red, pink, yellow or white flowers in summer. Plants grow about 1–3 feet high and must have a rich, moist soil. Cut off dead heads in autumn.

It likes more shade than sun.

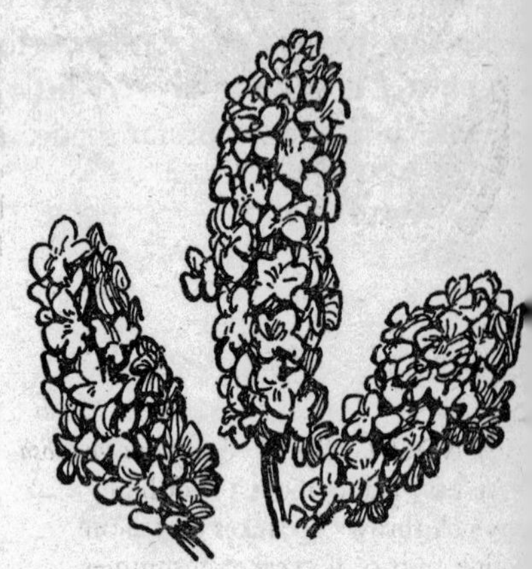

GARLAND FLOWER *Daphne mezereum*

This will grow almost anywhere and produces wreaths of pinkish flowers in February and March which have a beautiful perfume. The leaves come later in the spring. This shrub should not be pruned.

It likes a semi-shady position and room to grow up to 4 feet.

IVY *Hedera*

There are many forms of tiny-leaved ivies with green, or variegated green, white and yellow leaves, which are ideal plants for growing on walls or between paving cracks. They stand lots of hard treatment and can be cut back in spring if they get out of hand.

It likes moisture and more shade than sun.

LILY OF THE VALLEY

Convallaria majalis

Its stems carry sweetly scented, bell-shaped flowers, among long shiny leaves, early every summer. The plants like a rich soil and spread very quickly, so they have to be thinned out every year or so. Each autumn a layer of peat should be put over them. Keep them watered, but not too much.

It likes a semi-shady position.

LONDON PRIDE *Saxifraga umbrosa*

An easy plant, about 1 foot high, which throws up spikes of delicate pink tufts of flowers each summer among rosettes of glossy leaves.

It likes either sun or partial shade. It is not fussy about soil.

PENNYROYAL AND MINIATURE MINT — *Mentha pulegium and Mentha requienii*

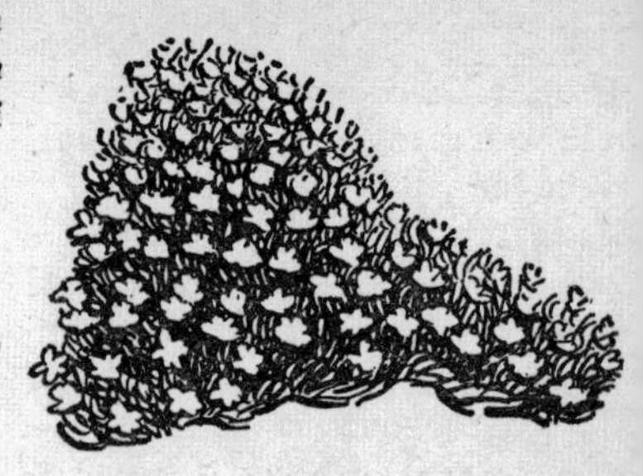

Both are ideal 'carpeting' plants with peppermint-smelling leaves and tiny flowers in summer. They will clamber anywhere among and over stones, and can even become a nuisance if not kept cut back.

It likes sun or shade.

PLANTAIN LILY — *Hosta*

This plant is grown mainly for its decorative leaves of green, white and yellow. Flowers of white or violet grow above the leaf 'tufts' during the summer. Dig up and divide in half every year or two.

It likes a shady place and rich, moist soil.

ST JOHN'S WORT — *Hypericum*

Bushy plant with masses of green leaves, and handsome yellow flowers like huge buttercups for a long time during the summer. It grows 1–2 feet high, spreads densely, and should be cut back in spring if it grows too big.

It likes a dryish soil, in either sun or shade.

SOLOMON'S SEAL *Polygonatum*
This grows about 2–3 feet tall and produces arching sprays of greenish and ivory bell-like flowers in early summer.

It likes really dense shade and really moist soil.

SPINDLE TREE *Euonymus*
This family of trees and shrubs grows to various heights from about 3 feet to 15 feet, but they can be pruned each spring to keep them the size you want for hedging, climbing, shrub or tree. The leaves turn lovely red colours in autumn before falling, and there are generally little pink or white berries as well. Some evergreen sorts stay green all winter, but they are not so decorative in autumn.

It likes any condition, shade or sun.

Some climbers

Buy a young plant in a pot (any time except winter), make a hole as big as the pot and 15 inches from the wall (or in a container 1–2 feet wide), remove the plant from the pot as on page 52, and put it in. Press compost well down and water thoroughly.

CLEMATIS ***Clematis***

There are lots of different kinds with beautiful, big flowers in many colours, and sometimes evergreen leaves. It produces more flowers if, after its first year, you prune it early in spring before it flowers. This means cutting off all the old dead bits and straggly shoots. In summer, give lots of water and fertilizer. In spring, give it bone meal.

It likes shade or sun, but must have its roots in shade: if necessary, put a few stones round the bottom.

CLIMBING HYDRANGEA ***Hydrangea petiolaris***

This hydrangea will grow anywhere, with big, flat, round clusters of white flowers in summer. If you want it to grow high, don't prune; but cutting off straggly stems makes better flowers next year. Train shoots round strings to go where you want.

It likes shade, and a little sun, with well-drained but moist soil. Don't put it against a south-facing wall.

COTONEASTER *Cotoneaster*

This has neat, shiny little leaves, white flowers and brilliant red berries in autumn. Most varieties keep their leaves on through winter and need no pruning.

It likes cool, shady places.

FIRETHORN *Pyracantha*

An evergreen with little white flowers in spring and summer, and bunches of bright orange berries in autumn. Don't prune it, but arrange its branches to go the way you want. It grows slowly.

It likes shade or sun.

HONEYSUCKLE *Lonicera*

An ornamental flower in summer, sweet-scented, particularly in the evening, in pinky-orangey colours. When the flowers die, cut their heads off – unless you want red berries later – to help more flowers to come. Give lots of water. Plant it to climb over a tree or arch, not just straight up. Evergreen types should be pruned in spring to the shape you want; those that drop their leaves need only tidying up.

It likes sun or shade, but must have its roots in shade.

JASMINE — *Jasminum*

The hardy winter jasmine (*nudiflorum*) produces starry yellow little flowers from late autumn till April, before leaves appear. Jasmines that flower later are sweet-scented: white, pink or yellow. Unless you want it to keep growing upwards, cut back each stem that has flowered, and cut off all side shoots that you don't want.

It likes shade more than sun.

JEW'S MALLOW — *Kerria japonica*

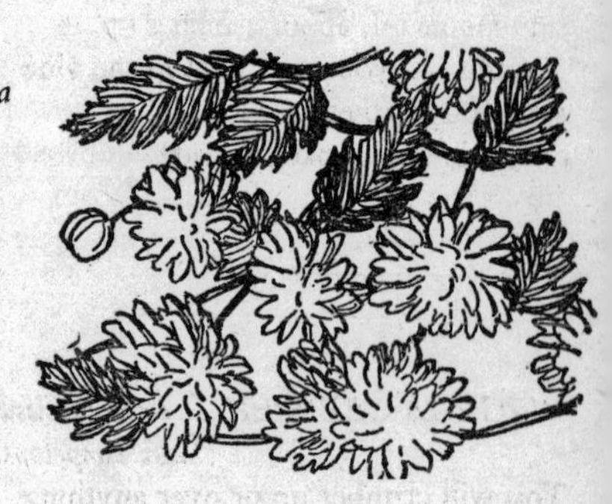

Prettily shaped, light-green leaves, bright-green stems and twinkling yellow flowers in spring. If it gets straggly, prune bits off after it has flowered. When it is 2–3 years old, you can dig it up (gently) and divide it in two to make two plants.

It likes either shade or sun.

MILE-A-MINUTE (RUSSIAN VINE) — *Polygonum baldschuanicum*

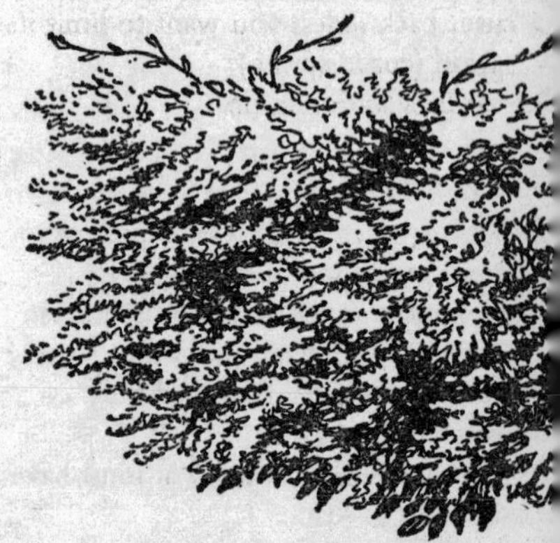

So-called because it can grow 15 feet in one year! It rampages up and over walls, sheds, etc, and is covered with a frothy mass of creamy-pink flowers from July to October. Cut it back a lot in autumn, or else you will have a jungle of it.

It likes shade or sun.

VINE *Vitis*

The flowers are nothing much to look at, but smell sweetly, and the leaves turn red and orange in autumn when purple-black berries appear (don't eat them). Cut the side shoots off, about 4 inches up, in autumn – if you want to stop the vine spreading further.

It likes sun or partial shade.

VIRGINIA CREEPER *Parthenocissus* and *Ampelopsis*

This will clamber up or over anything. It has particularly fine leaves, shiny and (in autumn) bright red and yellow. Don't cut it back unless you want to limit its spread (cut in spring).

It likes sun or shade.

Some ferns

Most ferns like damp and shade, and remain green all the year.

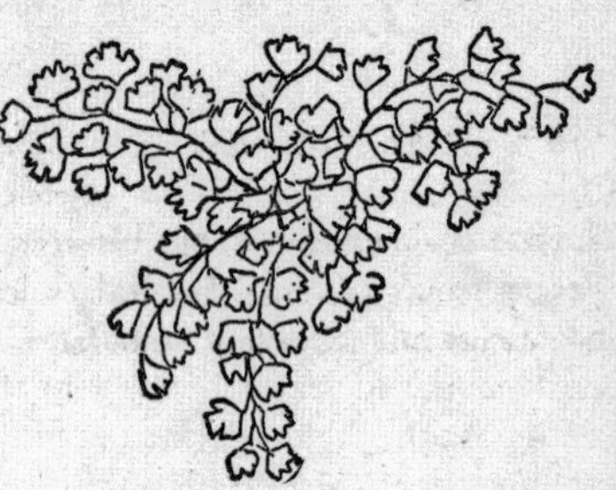

HARDY MAIDENHAIR *Adiantum venustum*

Beautiful little plant with tiny, lacy leaves, sometimes tinted brown when young. Fine for planting between stones. Six inches tall. Likes sun or shade, not too much damp.

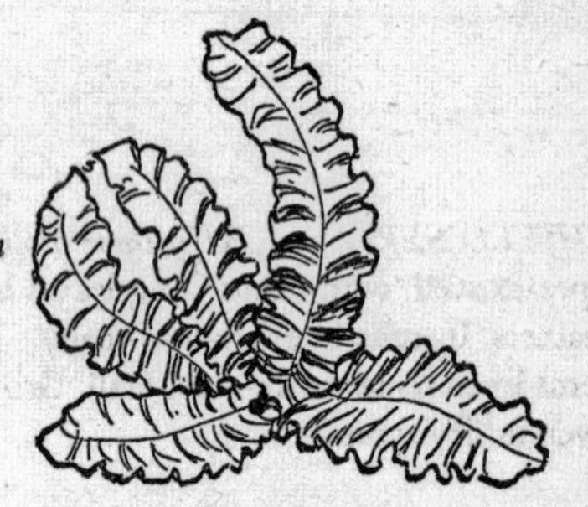

HART'S TONGUE *Phyllitis scolopendrium*

Wide, rippling, evergreen leaves of a rich green in a rosette shape. 1 foot tall.

MALE FERN *Dryopteris felix-mas*

A common but elegant fern, with divided lacy leaves, often remaining green all the year, 2–3 feet high. It spreads well.

It likes sun or shade, wet or dry.

NEW ZEALAND FERN *Blechnum penna marina*

A little creeping fern to put between paving stones or rocks. Small dark leaves, 2–3 inches tall, spreading quite far.

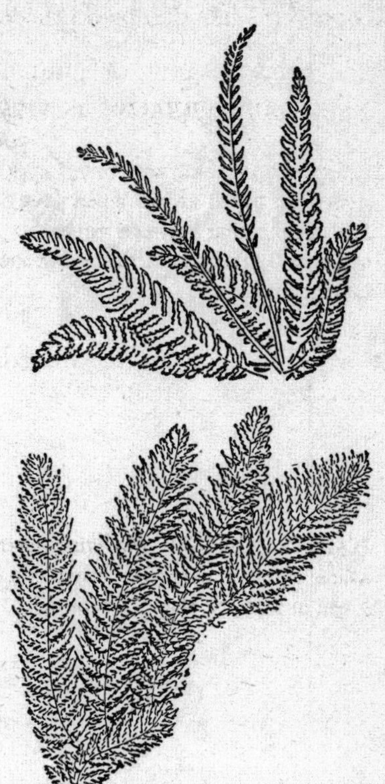

SHIELD FERN *Polystichum proliferum*

Spreads well, with dainty long leaves like feathers. It sometimes sends up baby ferns from its roots. 1½–2 feet tall. Grows even in dry spots.

How to divide one plant into two

Many plants grow into a miniature jungle, and need splitting up occasionally – whether they are in pots or in a garden. Do this in spring or autumn. Start by digging the plant up, or turning it out of its pot (*see* page 52).

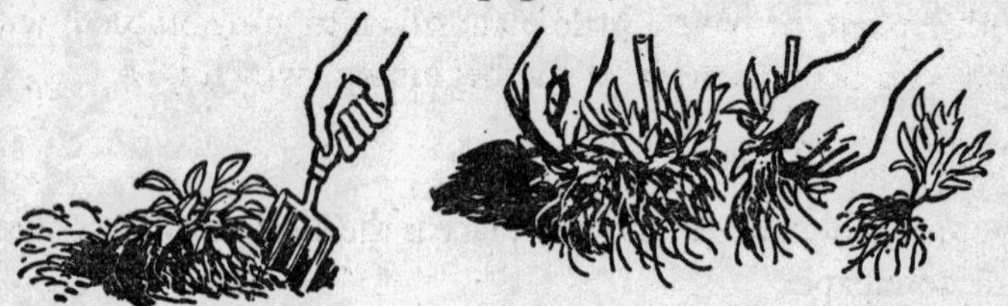

Put the clump on the ground

If it is small, hold the main part with one hand and with the other pull off side shoots and roots all round. Throw away the middle, and plant the rest in two or three places.

If the clump is too thick to pull apart without breaking roots and stems, cut it up with an old knife and plant the best bits.

A cluster of tubers or rhizomes can be pulled apart. Cut each into pieces, and every piece should start a new plant from the 'eyes'.

A cluster of bulbs can be pulled apart and replanted in small groups or individually.

No 10 Pot-plants Indoors

Lots of plants for the house are sold already in pots, and all you have to do is put them in the kind of place they like, water them, and so on. But if you are going to take a cutting from another plant, or have a little plant given to you complete with roots, you need to begin at the beginning, which is:

Finding a work-space

If your mother agrees, the best place is the kitchen table covered with newspaper.

Choosing a pot

Ordinary flowerpots with drainage holes in the bases used always to be made of red clay, but now plastic ones are more common. They are cheap, lightweight, and water does not evaporate from them so quickly.

On the other hand, with a clay pot it is easier to tell when watering is needed: you just tap it with a pencil or thumb-nail and tell by the sound! If all is well, it makes a dull sound; but if it makes a higher, ringing tone, water is needed. For plants that like soil to be a bit dry, clay pots would be better.

You can make your own pots out of old cream-cartons or foil pudding-basins if you pierce drainage holes in them. Old china bowls and mugs can be used but, with no drainage holes, they will need a layer of charcoal chips to absorb any surplus water that might otherwise make the compost sour (this could rot the plants' roots). Alternatively, drill holes in these also.

Crocks

So that the soil does not clog up the drainage hole, a layer of crocks goes in at the bottom. Crocks could be bits of broken clay flowerpots or china, pebbles, bits of broken brick (but not mortar because the lime in this kills some plants). Or even crumpled-up foil or bottle-tops.

Compost

John Innes Compost No 1 does for most plants. No 2 is richer and should be used for big plants or ones that will be left in the same pot for 2–3 years (which these are is mentioned later).

Putting the plant in

The important thing is not to crumple up the roots of a plant, so the pot should be big enough to avoid this; but if it is too large it makes the plant look measly, and the roots grow too much and take energy needed by the leaves and flowers.

Tip a layer of compost into the bottom of the pot. Then hold the plant or cutting in one hand in the centre with the roots well below where the surface of the compost will be. With the other hand, pour in compost, gently pushing it around the plant with your fingers. When the pot is nearly full, press the compost down firmly to hold the plant. Lightly spray the leaves and water the compost to settle it down.

Cuttings from bigger plants

If you are putting in a leaf or other cutting from a bigger plant, do this in spring and cover the pot with a transparent plastic bag supported on twigs till you see the new stems and leaves are under way. Then remove the bag. If the plant is very tender-looking, it may be sensible to replace the bag lightly over the young plants each night or on cold days for a week or so.

Mixing plants

In a large pot or bowl you could put more than one plant (provided they like the same amount of warmth, water, etc) but remember how they will grow. Plants tend to be of four kinds: tall or bushy, climbers-up or trailers-down. A low, trailing plant and a tall one might be happy together, but two tall ones might compete, and would not make such a decorative combination. Remember also that plants tend to lean towards the light, and to keep them straight you may have to turn the bowl every week or so. This means that whichever plant was at the back will now be at the front.

An alternative is to keep each plant in its own small pot, and put all the pots in one big bowl (or plant-trough, or box, or plastic-lined basket) tucking moss or peat into the spaces between. Then you can rearrange the assortment whenever you wish, and you can mix plants with different watering needs.

Most plants don't like a cool or dry atmosphere, and like their pots to be in a bigger container with damp peat round them. Or the pots could stand on a tray with a layer of pebbles or gravel, plus water just up to the surface of the gravel, which will evaporate and make the air round the plants moist. This is called creating a micro-climate – a small area within the bigger climate of the room as a whole.

Watering and care

Each pot, if not in an outer container, should stand on a saucer (or you could use foil pans or the little white trays in which supermarkets sell meat), or a group of them could stand on a tray in order to catch drips.

During summer, water most plants regularly as described on page 24, remembering to add liquid fertilizer as required (page 28), generally at least weekly. In hot weather, fill a plastic squeezy bottle, well rinsed out, with water to spray lightly on the leaves. During winter, less water is generally required – plants which need more are listed at the end of this chapter.

If you forget to water, the soil may shrink or cake hard so that ordinary water runs off it. If this happens, soak the pot in the sink for a quarter of an hour then leave it to drain for half an hour before returning it to its position.

You may get greenfly or other insects or diseases on your plants, in which case consult Chapter 12. Keep leaves clean by lightly rubbing with damp cotton wool.

Let all plants have plenty of fresh air, but not draughts: stand them outdoors during summer if you can.

Re-potting

If plants get too big, you can cut them back with scissors (do this at the end of summer); or, in the case of climbing types, you can give them sticks and strings to climb up, the latter fastened to something suitable like the end of a bookcase.

Most plants need to be put into bigger pots as they grow older. The signs are that they will wilt, cease growing leaves and push their roots through the drainage hole if they are too cramped.

In the case of others, remove them in late spring and not when in flower. How to do this was shown on page 110. Have ready a larger pot (with crocks) into which to put the ball of soil you have removed. Put some compost in the bottom, hold the ball in position, and fill with more compost round the edges, pressing well down.

Put the pot in a sink of water for a quarter of an hour, drain and put in a shady place for a week before moving it to its final home.

The plant may look droopy at first but should soon perk up. Lightly spray the leaves with water each morning.

Plants that are rarely re-potted should, after two years, have the top two inches of old compost replaced with new, taking care not to disturb the roots. Remember to fertilize when watering.

Choosing plants

The most important thing is to find plants that will suit your room – is it warm or cool, sunny or shady? Read the descriptions on page 116 and pick out plants that suit your rooms.

Only some plants have pretty flowers. But leaves alone can be attractive. There are so many different shapes, and some leaves have several colours in them – all the year round. Many flowering plants are useless once the flowers are over and the leaves drop. This applies to many flowers sold in pots at florists' shops – cyclamens, gloxinias, calceolarias, etc. Though useful for short periods of colourful display, they may or may not flower again if you put them in a garden; they really need to be in a greenhouse.

A lot of pot plants at Woolworth's and other shops come from a firm called Rochfords; they put a pink label on the ones that are easy to grow, so look out for these. (You can write to Rochfords for a free leaflet on house plants – their address is Turnford Hall, Broxbourne, Herts.)

You can buy these plants at any time of year (but if you are trying to raise your own plants from cuttings it is best to do this in spring). See that they are wrapped up before carrying them home in cold or windy weather. In hot weather, keep even the sun-loving plants out of the sun for a few days to let them settle in their new home and form new roots, shoots and leaves.

Plants for problem places

If you have an extra-sunny room, choose plants such as flame-nettle, busy Lizzie, geraniums, cacti or succulents. But try to keep the roots cool: you could put foil round the pots.

If you have a very dark room, choose ferns, fittonia, baby's tears, or ivy.

If it is very dry because you have central heating: spider plant, rubber plant, aluminium plant, mother-in-law's tongue, wandering Jew or cactus.

If there is a gas fire: busy Lizzie, or any thick-leaved plants.

If the room gets cold at night: kangaroo vine, fat-headed Lizzie, Japanese aralia, ivy, mother-of-thousands, wandering Jew, ferns.

Growing pot-plants from seeds

There are a few plants which can be easily grown this way without having to separate out a whole mass of seedlings. A few were described in Chapter 1. Just press 2–3 seeds ½ inch down into a 3-inch pot of compost; keep this damp and lightly covered with foil till the shoots are ½ inch high, then let the light in. You will need to transfer each plant to a 6- or 9-inch pot later, to give it room for growth.

You could grow in this way any seeds that are large enough to plant singly (some are as fine as sand and can only be scattered). Examples are sweet pea, nasturtium, morning glory, black-eyed Susan, canary creeper, and the cup-and-saucer plant. All except the last are annuals (they flower the first year only). The cup-and-saucer plant goes on for years and can grow 10 feet long on strings or on a big wire loop 'planted' in its pot.

Some tiny seeds are now sold inside pellets, which makes them easy to handle singly and thus to plant in pots. There is more about all these in Chapter 12.

Fruit and vegetables in pots

You can even have great fun growing miniature tomatoes and strawberries in pots indoors.

Buy a little alpine strawberry plant or the variety called Gento in the autumn, and put it in a 9-inch pot. Its runners will trail down with little white flowers and, later next summer, delicious fruit.

Tiny Tim tomatoes can be grown from little plants or from seeds as above, in the spring; or else get a packet of 'mixed ornamental' tomato seeds – they will produce all sorts of shapes, yellow or red, very good to eat as well as fascinating to look at.

Cucumbers of a special kind, called 'apple' because that is their shape, can also be grown like the tomatoes. The cucumbers are white.

All these plants need particular care over watering and fertilizing. They will last only one year.

An excellent little book to buy if you are going to have lots of house plants is *Be your own house plant expert* by D. G. Hessayon (15p, on sale from bookshops and gardening shops).

All the plants in Chapter 2 can also be grown in pots, and those in Chapters 3, 5 (indoor ones), 6, 7 (indoor ones) and 8 (indoor ones).

BIRD'S NEST FERN *Asplenium nidus*
A pretty little fern with graceful, arching leaves, green all the year. Baby plantlets on its fronds can be carefully detached and planted.

It likes warmth but doesn't mind shade.

DRAGON PLANT *Dracaena*
A tall plant with long, striped leaves. Water its leaves and the compost well in summer. To divide the plant, cut a stem into pieces in spring and put in compost, in a warm room, with a transparent plastic bag over it.

It likes a warm room, either light or shady.

FAT-HEADED LIZZIE *Fatshedera lizei*

Not a real ivy, though the leaf is similar in shape, and leathery. Nip the top buds off as it grows, to keep it a bushy shape. To start, take one shoot and put it in compost. Water well in summer, and wipe leaves clean.

It likes warmth.

FIG *Ficus*

Lots of varieties, including a climbing one. *F.elastica decora* is known as the rubber-plant and has shiny, big leaves. *F.pumila* is the smaller, climbing fig. (Neither grows figs – or rubber!) To start a new one, take a piece of stem with a leaf on and plant it, keeping it warm and moist. Keep the leaves clean.

It likes warmth but not much sun, and no draughts.

FLAME-NETTLE *Coleus*

Very ornamental leaves of mixed red, yellow, white and green. Give it plenty of water and nip off the tips to make it grow bushy. These tips can be planted to make new plants for next spring.

It likes lots of light, no draughts, warmth, and moist air.

INDOOR PRIMROSE *Primula*

There are several kinds, with white, pink, purple or reddish clusters of flowers in winter or spring, above a rosette of roundish leaves. After flowering, keep it in a cool, shady place during summer, then bring it into the light and give it plenty of water (with fertilizer) in late summer, for a second crop of flowers. But it is unlikely to flower another year.

It likes an airy but not draughty room, not too much sun or warmth.

IVY ARUM *Scindapsus*

Not a real ivy, but it does climb. Green and yellow marbled leaves. Take one leaf and a piece of stem to put in compost.

It likes light and warmth, without draughts, and should never dry out.

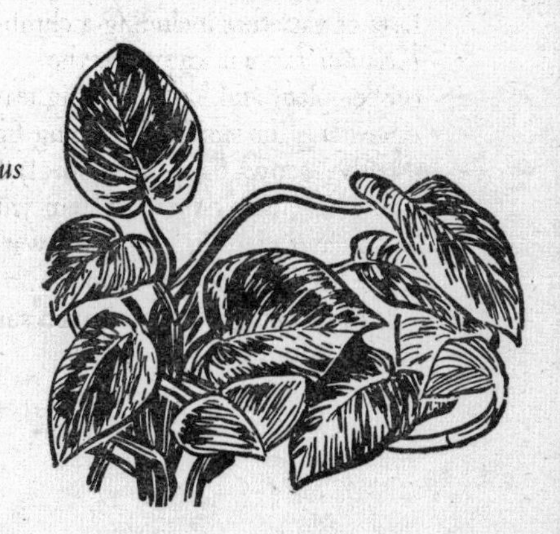

JAPANESE ARALIA *Fatsia japonica*

Big leathery leaves. As it grows, nip the top buds off – then it will grow into a nice bushy shape. To start, take one shoot to put in sand mixed with compost in a warm place. It needs plenty of water in summer and its leaves should be cleaned regularly.

It likes a cool and shady room.

JASMINE *Jasminum polyanthum*

This is an indoor variety: a climbing plant with sweet-scented, yellow-white flowers and little green leaves. It can be trained round canes or up strings. The older shoots should be cut off when the plant gets overcrowded, and the bottom pieces of these can start new plants.

It likes a warm room and sunshine – no draughts.

KANGAROO VINE *Cissus antarctica*

This one will climb if you give it string for its tendrils to grip. Take a stem with one leaf to put in compost, and keep warm.

It likes a room that is not too hot or dry. It will put up with shade and some draughts.

MAIDENHAIR FERN *Adiantum*

Tiny, flimsy leaves on delicate stalks. Give it plenty of water. One plant can make two by dividing the roots (*see* page 110).

It likes a shady room, with no gas fumes or draughts.

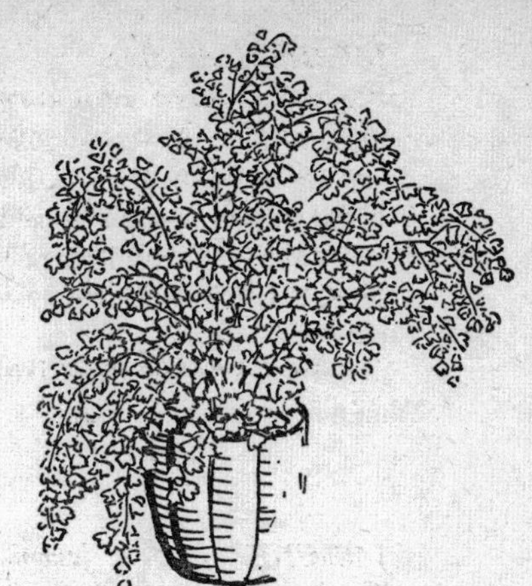

PRAYER PLANT *Maranta*

The leaves are decorated with brown and pink splashes. They fold up at night as if kneeling in prayer. Divide one plant into two as on page 110.

It likes a warm but shady room without draughts, and it must not be dry.

PTERIS FERN *Pteris*

There are lots of different kinds, with varying colours and leaf-shapes. One plant can be divided in two (*see* page 110).

It likes a shady room, with no gas fumes or draughts, and some warmth in winter.

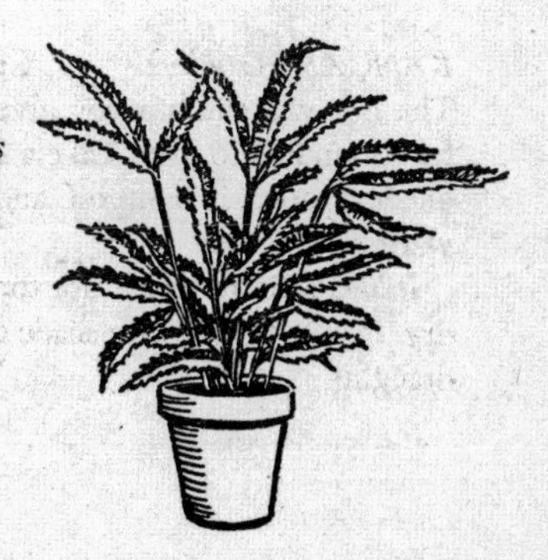

SILK OAK *Grevillea robusta*

Nothing like an oak! The feathery leaves on this tall plant are silvery and silky underneath, and it sometimes has yellow flowers. Cut the branches shorter in spring.

It likes light and coolness; an airy place, but not draughty.

UMBRELLA PLANT *Cyperus*

Long, grassy leaves on short stems. For new plants, divide the roots in spring as on page 110. Give it lots of water and keep it in a saucer of water.

It likes shade and does not mind cold.

WINTER CHERRY *Solanum*

A little shrub with red-orange berries in winter (they're not real cherries – don't eat them). The berries can last for months if in the right conditions. Cut it back to a neat shape in spring and give it a holiday outdoors. New plants will grow from shoots cut off in spring and planted. Water and fertilize it regularly.

It likes light, but no draughts or gas fumes.

No 11 Scents and Flavours

Looking, touching, listening, smelling and tasting – these are your five senses and you can use and enjoy them all in gardening.

Looking means more than just enjoying the pretty spectacle of flowers in bloom. It means real observation – it takes a keen eye to notice a slight change in the colour of a leaf which may tell you the plant needs more water (or less), less sunlight (or more), or just that autumn is coming. How good are you at spotting the very first tiny leaf-buds on a stem? or noticing a deadly insect only $\frac{1}{20}$ inch long and removing it or killing it with an insecticide before it does harm? It is fascinating to watch roots growing from plants in jars of water – some long, fleshy and few; others a mass of fine winding hairs. Look out for fungus attacking a plant, no more visible than a cobweb or a greyish patch – cut it out and burn it.

It is fascinating to observe young plants develop from tiny seedlings, to spot the variations between different sorts of the same plant, to peer inside a flower and study all the different parts, to watch insects pollinating them.

Touching (but gently) is important too. If you know the springy feel of your plants' leaves when they are fit, you will soon recognize the flabbiness that means all is not well, so that you can quickly change the warmth, moisture, etc, they are getting, in the hope of restoring them. Touch tells you a lot about the soil and compost, too – whether it is too hard and caked, too wet and slimy, or too dry (and elsewhere this book tells you what to do to put such matters right). It is also fascinating to feel, very gently, the differences in texture of flowers, stems and leaves. Some are smooth and shiny, others rough and prickly, some are velvety or silky, some hard and others soft.

Listening – yes, even that comes into gardening! You will learn to recognize from a tap on the pot the ringing sound that means water may be urgently needed. Wind, too, should be listened for: it can make a lovely swishing noise among plants, but it is also a warning sometimes to tie your taller plants to a stick in case a gale is on its way, which may break them. Other plant noises to listen for are things like the bursting open of seed pods – particularly the bigger ones like sweet peas or wild poppies. If you gently press the central coloured tube of a fuchsia flower, it will pop as it bursts open. Bulbs sometimes make a scratchy noise like mice when the flowers are opening in warmth and the buds push the leaves aside to make room for themselves.

Smelling is one of the senses we are in danger of neglecting. Dogs and other animals use their noses to good effect, but we tend to think about ours only when we've got a cold or there's a nasty smell about. The scents of many flowers and leaves (particularly if rubbed between your fingers) are as rich and pleasurable as colours, and, for blind people, some parks have special gardens filled only with the most fragrant plants. If you enjoy smelling flowers and leaves, then choose from the following list (the numbers in brackets refer to the chapters in this book where you will find out more about them). Unfortunately, some varieties of flowers don't have the fragrance of others: ask about this when you buy.

Honeysuckle (9)
Hyacinth (2)
Jasmine (9)
Lily – some kinds (8)
Lily of the valley (9)
Narcissus – some kinds (8)
Pennyroyal (9)
Sweet pea (12)

Nasturtium – most kinds (10)
Chives, Parsley, Rosemary, Sage } especially when rubbed (11)
Begonia (some kinds) (2)
Geranium (some kinds) (2)
Fuchsia (some kinds) (5)

Pelargonium (some kinds) (5)	Garland Flower (9)
Australian violet (7)	Mint (9)
Thyme (7)	Clematis (some kinds) (9)
Camomile (7)	Night scented stock (12)
Miniature rose (some kinds) (7)	

You will notice that most give off their scent when the sun is on them, but honeysuckle is at its best in the evening or after a warm shower of rain.

Tasting is another great pleasure of gardening. A number of fruits and vegetables are described in other chapters (1, 10). Home-grown ones always taste much better than those from shops. Don't forget, either, that certain plants usually grown only for their looks can also be eaten in salads – nasturtiums and dandelion leaves especially. Don't experiment with others, though – for some plants are poisonous.

One of the tastiest kinds of plants used in cooking are herbs, and you should be very popular with your mother if you create a little herb garden from which she can take pieces of the plants to put in stews and other dishes she is cooking – or you might like to try them out yourself if you like cooking. The next page describes five you can grow in pots outdoors or on the kitchen windowsill (if it is cool and light), in addition to mint for boiling with potatoes or making into mint sauce, which was described in Chapter 1 (it can grow in compost or in water, as you prefer).

When you want some to use, cut a stem off close to the bottom, rinse well, and chop into tiny bits with scissors before mixing it into the dish to be cooked.

Grow herbs in pots with John Innes Compost No 1 or No 2. You could put a row of pots in a plant trough. Start them off in spring.

CHIVES
The 'baby' of the onion family, with a more delicate flavour in its grass-like leaves which live on for year after year. Buy a clump and plant as described on page 112. Chop and sprinkle the leaves into mashed potato, scrambled eggs, cream cheese, soup or salad. Water it well, and divide in two after 2–3 years.

It likes any light spot.

PARSLEY
This can make a decorative, bright-green, frilly edge to a flowerbed, though winter frost may kill it there. But a plant can be bought to keep in a pot, and may last more than one year. Cut only a few stems at a time: if you take the lot, the plant will stop growing. Chop and sprinkle in white sauce (to go with fish or chicken), on top of stew or soup, in scrambled egg, or on boiled potatoes. Give it lots of water.

It likes a light spot.

ROSEMARY
A little shrub, living on for years, with small blue flowers in summer on stems of spiky leaves which should be cut back by two-thirds when flowering is over. Trim it if it gets straggly. You can grow a bush from just one cutting put in during spring. Chop the leaves and sprinkle on lamb or chicken before grilling or roasting it.

It likes sunshine and well-drained soil or compost.

SAGE
This has broad leaves of soft green. You can start a plant from a 2-inch piece of the original stem in spring. In June, before it flowers, cut half the stems off and hang upside down to dry in a warm, airy place, for use later in the year (you can do this with other herbs, too). This goes well with pork or sausages, or with onion in a stuffing for chicken or duck, or with liver. A little goes a long way. As the years go by, cut out old stems if it gets big.

It likes sunshine. Soil should not be soggy, even though sage likes being watered.

THYME
A little bush that goes on from year to year, and can be started from a cutting with a bit of root on it, in spring. You can take stems throughout summer and strip the tiny leaves off to use or to dry. It goes well in stuffings and stews; try sprinkling it on tomatoes, too, before grilling them – or on fish. Water very little.

It likes sunshine and well-drained soil or compost.

No 12 Growing Plants From Seeds

Seeds are the principal way in which plants reproduce themselves. Within each seed is a microscopic shoot and root, with a store of food for them to live on, and these are protected by a hard shell which has to crack open before they can emerge into the soil. All seeds need to go through a ripening period and sometimes this may be very short, as with pansies, but in others it may be months or years. In most cases germination happens only after winter's frost and rain have softened the seed shell and spring's warmth has encouraged the new plant to start growing. First the root appears, and then the shoot, and when that has happened you have a seedling.

Most seeds want darkness at first, also moisture, air and warmth; and this is why it is usually best to start seeds off in the spring. And because not all seeds will succeed in growing, nature usually scatters an abundance of them around.

When you buy a packet of seeds, you may get hundreds smaller than a grain of sand, or a few the size of small peas. The very fine ones are troublesome to use if you have only a few pots or plant troughs for your 'garden' (you get hundreds of seedlings which have to be separated and replanted), so it is better to stick to the larger seeds which can be planted three or four to a 6–10 inch pot and left there. Or they can be planted singly in 4-inch pots and moved into bigger ones as their main homes later.

Keep a lookout for packets of 'pelleted' seeds in the shops. These are ones that have been prepared by taking very fine seeds and enclosing them in a coating of fertilized material, so that you can pick them up and plant them individually just like the naturally big seeds. You may get as many as 150 to a packet, so you will probably have plenty to share with friends. Don't expect every one to produce a plant, though.

The seeds recommended for growing in pots on pages 133–5 are all naturally big ones and so are easy to handle. Amongst the pelleted seeds generally available, the following are suitable for pots: ageratum, alyssum, aster, candytuft, clarkia, pansy, godetia, cornflower, night-scented stock (small varieties only), petunia, larkspur, love-in-a-mist, viscaria, viola. These are all annuals; the seeds can be sown in spring and will grow and flower that summer.

Packets of seeds generally carry pictures of the flowers and instructions for growing them, so you can see before you buy which are suited to the spot you have in mind – indoors or out, sunny or shady – and when to plant them. Don't mix types with different needs.

Before sowing your seeds, first of all prepare the pots. They must have drainage holes in them, and make sure they are clean. Place a 1-inch layer of crocking material (kitchen foil, broken pots, small stones, etc) at the base, then fill firmly to within 1½ or 2 inches of the top with John Innes Compost No 1. Then put the seeds on the surface about 2 inches apart. Sprinkle a little compost over the top (enough to cover the seeds – the bigger the seeds the more soil they need on top of them), and sprinkle on a little water. Pop a transparent plastic bag over the top, and on top of this a brown paper bag or a 'hat' of newspaper. The plastic bag will keep moisture from evaporating, and the brown one will keep light out.

Alternatively, you can buy transparent plastic domes (some sold in plant shops, some in hardware shops for covering food), or you may have a transparent plastic box that was used for packaging chocolates, etc, and either of these – or even a glass jar – would do instead of the plastic bag; but cover it with paper or foil for darkness.

When the pots of seeds have been prepared, either stand them outdoors in a warm shady place if the plants are of the kind that only require outdoor conditions, or place them in the warmest place you can find in your home – airing cupboard, kitchen, bathroom, for example – if they are the kind known as house plants which require constantly warmer conditions.

Once the seedlings are visible, you can throw the brown bag away and let them enjoy the light. But leave the plastic bag to protect the seedlings – keep it off them by supporting it on twigs or wire.

About watering. At first, use a pepperpot or sugar sprinkler – otherwise, a flood of water could wash the seeds out of the compost. Water about twice a week. Later, be more generous. Add fertilizer to the water only when the plants have grown past the seedling stage and produced several leaves.

When you have a full-size plant, you treat it in the usual way, as described earlier in this book.

Sometimes, the instructions on the packet tell you to chip the coating off the seeds before you plant them, to help the seedling emerge. Place each seed on a kitchen chopping-board, and press firmly down with a sharp knife – mind your fingers, and also mind the little 'scar' on the side of the seed. This is where the shoot is, and it should not be cut, so chop on the other side. An alternative to chipping is to soak the seeds for a day.

Growing from seeds needs patience. Even in the best weather outdoors, or the most suitable conditions indoors, it may be months before you see a shoot and even longer before a plant has grown. Generally, however, you can expect most seedlings to appear in 7–21 days. Some plants – the annuals – grown from seeds flower one year only. You will have to start all over again if you want more next year. But very many others will grow and flower for many years to come: these are the perennials.

FLAMINGO FLOWER *Anthurium*
(perennial)
The glossy red flower with a 'tail' in the middle can grow three feet high, surrounded by evergreen leaves. Sow the seeds in spring with peat added to the compost. Water well in summer. Add more peat on top each spring. An indoor plant which should flower each year. Packets of five seeds available.

It likes constant warmth, no draughts, and shade.

GIANT SUNFLOWER *Helianthus*
(annual)
This monster will grow 6–10 feet tall, so it needs to go into the garden or a huge pot, outdoors or in, with a stick to which to tie it. Its big yellow flowers, packed with seeds, appear late in summer. Plant the seeds in April, and give it fertilizer when watering all through the summer. Packets of about 25 seeds.

It likes lots of sun.

GOURD, ORNAMENTAL *Cucurbita*
(annual)
Seeds should be sown about May, either outdoors where they are to grow or in pots indoors. Allow the plants space to scramble over the ground, or train them up wires or string. They will produce lots of little hard fruits in all sorts of shapes and colours. Let them ripen fully before picking. They are not to eat, but make lovely decorations indoors for winter. Packets of about 10 seeds.

It likes sun and plenty of water with fertilizer.

KAFIR LILY *Clivia*
(perennial)
Among the long, strap-like, evergreen leaves will appear big showy clusters of orange or yellow flowers 1–2 feet tall. Sow the seeds in March. Water well in summer. It should flower the following year. Packets of three seeds available.

It likes summer warmth but should be kept cool in winter, and it likes sunshine.

NASTURTIUM, DWARF *Tropaeolum nanum*
(annual)
Trumpet-shaped flowers in flame colours, with pretty, round leaves of light green. Sow seeds by pushing them into the soil 1 inch deep, in late spring, outdoors, for summer flowers. It often seeds itself naturally in the garden. It can also be sown and kept indoors in a light, sunny position. Packets of about 12–30 seeds.

It likes sunshine and space to scramble.

SWEETHEART PLANT *Philodendron scandens*
(perennial)

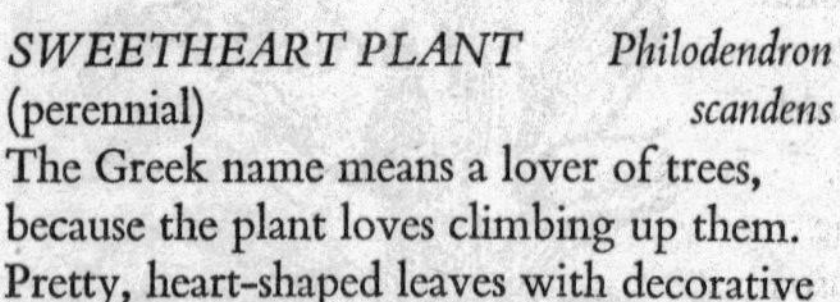

The Greek name means a lover of trees, because the plant loves climbing up them. Pretty, heart-shaped leaves with decorative veins. Water well. An indoor plant. Packets of five seeds available.

It likes warmth, if possible, shade, and no draughts.

SWEET PEA, DWARF *Lathyrus*
(annual)
Fragrant, delicate flowers – shades of purple, white, pink or red. Sow seeds in March in pots outdoors.
After the second pair of leaves has opened, pinch out between finger and thumb the tip of each main shoot. A week or so later, put the plants into the open ground or individual pots for flowering. Strip flowers off as soon as they fade, to encourage more. Give lots of water and fertilizer. If necessary, shelter them from wind. Can be grown indoors in pots, in light, sunny places. Packets of 12–30 seeds.
It likes plenty of sun.

URN PLANT *Aechmea*
(perennial)
The long, spiky green and silver leaves grow in a rosette and form a kind of vase in the middle (where a pink or red flower will grow 1–2 feet tall). This vase should be kept filled with water, plus a little fertilizer in summer, and the soil should also be kept damp if the room is hot. The plant will produce 'babies' at the sides before it dies and these can be used for new plants. An indoor plant. Packets of five seeds available.
It likes warmth, if possible, and shade.

Enemies of Pot-Plants

If leaves wither, drop, go grey or brittle, show strange dots or streaks – look to see whether insects are attacking them. Here are pictures of half a dozen that do harm (some others do good). They are arranged in order of approximate size – the first is as small as a grain of salt, so it's easy to miss; and even the last is not much bigger than a pin-head. Have you got a magnifying-glass?

1. *Red spider mite*
In a hot, dry room you may find minute, green-red mites underneath leaves, causing grey colouring.

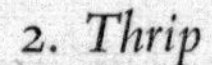

2. *Thrip*
Tiny, black flies that attack flowers and leaves, making them spotty.

3. *White fly*
A sticky dew on the plant may tell you when this moth-like fly is about, sucking the sap.

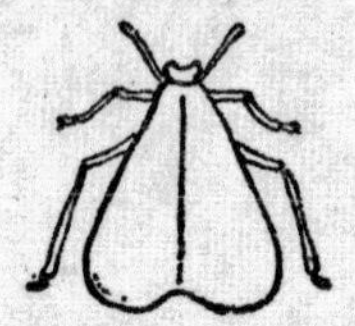

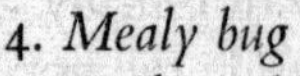

4. *Mealy bug*
Look under leaves and at stem joints during summer for this white, woolly-looking pest.

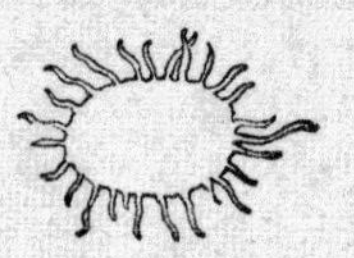

5. *Greenfly (Aphides)*
Look on young shoots and under leaves for clusters of them. They can be green or black.

6. *Scale insect*
Little waxy shells cling to stems and leaves, and create a sticky dew.

Scale insects and mealy bugs are so static that they can simply be scraped off: wrap the tip of a matchstick in cotton wool damped with methylated spirits. For the others, which run or fly, buy an aerosol of derris, or some liquid derris, and put it in a plastic squeezy-bottle to spray on, adding as much water as the label recommends. Though some insecticides (chemicals to kill insects) are poisonous to humans, this one is quite safe – except to any sort of fish, so cover these up if they are near.

There is another harmful insect you will easily recognize – the ant. Deal with him by getting some Panant and sprinkling a few drops outside the pots.

Plants can also get illnesses – rot or mould. All you can do then is cut off and burn the sick part so that the infection shan't spread, and also make sure you're growing the plants in the conditions they like most so that they can get well again.

Index

Piccolo General

Elizabeth Gundrey
SEWING THINGS (line illus) 25p

Jean Plaidy
THE YOUNG ELIZABETH (line illus) 20p
THE YOUNG MARY QUEEN OF SCOTS (line illus) 20p

Margaret Powell
SWEETMAKING FOR CHILDREN (line illus $7\frac{1}{2}'' \times 5''$) 20p

Marguerite Patten
JUNIOR COOK BOOK (line illus $7\frac{1}{2}'' \times 5''$) 25p
HOW: General Knowledge Question and Answer Book 20p

Puzzles and Games

Jack Cox
FUN AND GAMES OUTDOORS (illus) 20p
FUN AND GAMES INDOORS (illus) 20p

K. Franken
PUZZLERS FOR YOUNG DETECTIVES (illus) 20p

Tom Robinson
PICCOLO QUIZ BOOK (illus) 20p

Alfred Sheinwold
101 BEST CARD GAMES FOR CHILDREN (illus) 20p

Herbert Zim
CODES AND SECRET WRITING (illus) 20p

Robin Burgess
THE PICCOLO CROSSWORD BOOKS 1 to 8, each 20p

Norman G. Pulsford
THE PICCOLO PUZZLE BOOKS 1 to 8, each 20p

These and other PICCOLO Books are obtainable from all booksellers and newsagents. If you have any difficulty please send purchase price plus 7p postage to PO Box 11, Falmouth, Cornwall.
While every effort is made to keep prices low, it is sometimes necessary to increase prices at short notice. PAN Books reserve the right to show new retail prices on covers which may differ from those advertised in the text or elsewhere.